WOW IN SPACE

Mindy Thomas and Guy Raz
with Thomas van Kalken

Illustrated by Mike Centeno

Clarion Books

An Imprint of HarperCollins*Publishers*

To every one of our Wowzers here on Earth—
a galactic gush of gratitude to you for joining us on
all of our Wow in the World adventures —MT & GR

This illustrated intergalactic journey wouldn't have
been possible without the help and love of my two
favorite cosmonauts Anna and Rigby, as well as
the support of my friends and family. I hope these
drawings inspire all the Wowzers to look up at the
stars and find the universal wow. —MC

Clarion Books is an imprint of HarperCollins Publishers.

Wow in the World: Wow in Space

Text copyright © 2023 by Tinkercast LLC

Illustrations copyright © 2023 by Tinkercast LLC

Library of Congress Control Number: 2023933329

ISBN 978-0-35-869707-7

The artist used traditional pencils and pens, Photoshop, and a Wacom tablet
to create the mixed media illustrations for this book.

Typography by Abby Denning and Sarah Nichole Kaufman

23 24 25 26 27 COS 10 9 8 7 6 5 4 3 2 1

First Edition

CONTENTS

INTRODUCTION

CALLING ALL SPACE CADETS

We invite you and your imagination on an intergalactic, outer space vacation! We'll explore the solar system, see the stars, and experience life in a world just beyond ours.

What is out there?

How do we know?

Where in the galaxy do you want to go?

The who, what, when, where, how, and WOW of space—all in one place!

THE BIG BANG

How It All Began

Once upon a time, before time, before space, before light, before, well, *everything*, there was a teeny-tiny spot in the middle of pure nothingness. This spot was smaller than the smallest dot, and this spot was **HOT**.

ABOUT 500,000,000,000 TIMES SMALLER THAN THIS DOT

And crammed into this hot spot were the ingredients for everything that would make up the universe as we know it.

The pressure inside this little hot dot kept building and building until, nearly 14 billion years ago, in a split second . . .

It **BURST**.

Everything in the universe expanded and exploded into existence! At first, it was just a big hot mess of light and energy, but as the universe grew bigger, the temperature cooled. The cold turned that energy into more dots and spots that teamed up to form atoms, which make up almost everything in the universe. We're talking stars, cars, people, planets, socks, rocks, lakes, snakes, poop, soup, and even **YOU**.

At first, those atoms just made a huge cloud of .
But soon gravity started pulling it all together. Then, our baby universe began to form stars and galaxies, planets and moons too.

And this was only the beginning.

The universe is still

EXPANDING

every second of every day!

**THE UNIVERSE:
13.8 BILLION YEARS OLD**

THE SUN:
4.5 BILLION YEARS OLD

THE SOLAR SYSTEM:
4.5 BILLION YEARS OLD

LIFE ON EARTH:
3.5 BILLION YEARS OLD

UNIVERSE BUILDING 101

Congratulations on purchasing a Build Your Own Universe starter kit! Inside you'll find 118 different elements. These elements are the building blocks that make up everything in our universe, SO DON'T LOSE THEM!

To help keep track of all these elements, our in-house Russian chemist, Dmitri Mendeleev, has laid them out in a handy little guide called the periodic table. Check it out!

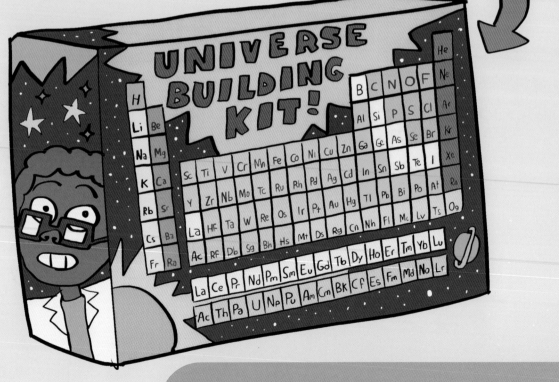

Remember, with your natural building blocks, the lightest element is **hydrogen** and the heaviest is **uranium**.

Some of these elements were made during the big bang, but a lot of them were created through celestial events known as supernovas. Supernovas happen at the end of a star's life cycle. Once a star has used up all its helium and hydrogen, it explodes!

This creates new, heavier elements.

Elements cannot be created or destroyed; they just get recycled! Every time an element gets recycled through a star's life cycle, heavier and heavier elements are created, such as gold and copper.

See, Mindy! Even stars know how to reuse, reduce, and recycle!

Every single element that is heavier than iron has passed through at least one **SUPERNOVA**.

Here is just one example of what you can make with our one-of-a-kind building kit!

WATER

Take two parts hydrogen and one part oxygen and presto—you've got a water molecule!

Construct another 1,500,000,000,000,000,000,000,000 of these molecules, and you'll have enough for a single drop of water!

1

2

3

4

Am I Made of Stardust?

Yes! It's most likely that close to 100 percent of the elements that make up *you*—from the oxygen in your lungs to the calcium in your bones to the iron in your blood—have passed through one or more supernovas! However, there is a teeny-tiny chance that some of the hydrogen in your body could have originated from the big bang itself!

HOW TO MAKE A GALAXY

THE GREAT UNIVERSAL BAKING SHOW

WELCOME TO **THE GREAT UNIVERSAL BAKING SHOW**! GUY RAZ, TELL THE VIEWERS WHAT WE'LL BE MAKING TODAY!

OUR VERY OWN GALAXY: COMPLETE WITH STARS, PLANETS, MOONS, AND ASTEROIDS.

SOUNDS YUMMY! LET'S GET STARTED!

SO, WHAT KIND OF GALAXY ARE WE MAKING TODAY, CHEF RAZ?

A galaxy is a huge collection of gas, dust, and stars held together by gravity. Galaxies can come in all shapes and sizes, from dwarf galaxies that contain a few hundred million stars to giant galaxies with more than a trillion stars.

WELL, MINDY, WE HAVE A FEW TO CHOOSE FROM.

THERE ARE THREE MAIN TYPES OF GALAXY FORMATIONS.

SPIRAL GALAXY
THESE GALAXIES ARE FLAT, BLUEISH WHITE, AND HAVE ARMS THAT FLARE OUT IN A CIRCULAR PINWHEEL SHAPE. TWO THIRDS OF OBSERVED GALAXIES ARE SPIRAL GALAXIES!

A Slice of Home

Our home galaxy, the Milky Way, is a spiral galaxy. It's approximately 100,000 light-years across and contains at least 100 billion stars.

ELLIPTICAL GALAXY

THESE MAKE UP ALMOST A FIFTH OF THE GALAXIES WE CAN SEE FROM EARTH. SOME ARE CIRCULAR, SOME ARE EGG-SHAPED, AND THEY COME IN ALL DIFFERENT SIZES—FROM DWARF ELLIPTICALS THAT ARE JUST 10,000 LIGHT-YEARS ACROSS TO HUGE GALAXIES MORE THAN A MILLION LIGHT-YEARS ACROSS.

IRREGULAR GALAXY

SOME GALAXIES CAN'T BE DEFINED BY THEIR SHAPE ALONE. IRREGULAR GALAXIES ARE MOST COMMONLY FOUND IN THE DEEPEST, OLDEST REGIONS OF SPACE. THAT MAKES SCIENTISTS THINK THEY WERE FORMED BEFORE GRAVITY WAS ABLE TO PULL THEM INTO SHAPE.

WE HAVE TO WAIT FOR THIS GALAXY TO BAKE!

HOW LONG SHOULD I SET THE TIMER FOR, BUDDY?

AROUND 500 MILLION YEARS!

WHAT?!

AFTER A FEW HUNDRED MILLION YEARS, THE GASES AND DARK MATTER START TO CLUSTER TOGETHER THANKS TO GRAVITY. AFTER A WHILE, THESE CLUSTERS BECOME SO DENSE, THEY COMBUST.

KIND OF LIKE POPCORN KERNELS IN THE MICROWAVE.

POP

YEAH!

WHEN THESE GASES COMBUST, THEY BECOME STARS!
THEN, THE GRAVITY OF THESE STARS ATTRACTS OTHER STARS.

NOW YOU'VE GOT A CLUSTER OF STARS.

AND THESE STAR CLUSTERS ATTRACT OTHER STAR CLUSTERS...

AND BEFORE YOU KNOW IT, YOU'VE GOT YOURSELF A GALAXY!

IT'S SO BEAUTIFUL

SCIENTISTS BELIEVE THAT THERE ARE MORE THAN 2 TRILLION GALAXIES IN OUR UNIVERSE... BUT THIS ONE IS JUST FOR US!

WHOA, THAT'S KIND OF HEAVY!

In our universe, planets, stars, and other celestial objects come in all shapes and sizes. Some are light enough to float in the ocean, whereas others are so heavy they bend light itself.

Look at them floating! They must be as light as balloons!

Actually, Guy Raz, nothing could be further from the truth!

OUR SUN

The sun is not only the largest object in our solar system (at 109 times wider than Earth), it's also the heaviest, making up 99.8 percent of the solar system's total mass.

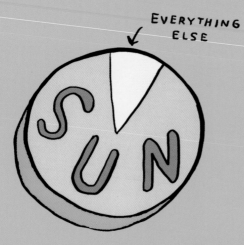

EVERYTHING ELSE

SUN

SOLAR SYSTEM'S WEIGHT

The sun weighs 4,385,000,000,000,000,000,000,000,000,000 pounds (1,989,000,000,000,000,000,000,000,000,000 kg) or, to put it into perspective, around 333,000 Earths. This is often referred to as 1 solar mass.

315 SOLAR MASSES

IGHING ATION

DOCK 1

RMC 136A1

RMC 136a1 is one of the most massive stars known to science. It lies about 163,000 light-years from Earth in the Tarantula Nebula. The star was discovered by South African astronomers in 1960 and is estimated to weigh more than 315 solar masses! Although this is the heaviest star known to date, scientists believe that it used to be even heavier . . . and has been dropping weight for the past few million years!

Galactic

TWO SOLAR MASSES

SMALL BUT MIGHTY

NEUTRON STAR

Neutron stars are some of the densest objects in the universe. Although they're typically only the size of a small city, they can weigh twice as much as the sun. Neutron stars are created when a much larger star runs out of gas and collapses in on itself before exploding in a massive celestial event known as a supernova.

Talk about going out with a bang!

These stars are so dense that a single teaspoon of a neutron star would weigh more than 1 billion tons (907 million metric tons)!

One of the larger neutron stars in our galaxy is called PSR J1614-2230.

Although it's only around 15 miles (24 km) wide, it has a weight of 2 solar masses!

Catchy name!

Whoa! That's like 2,204,622,621,849 pounds (1 million kg)! Or one Mount Everest!

66 BILLION SOLAR MASSES

IGHING
ATION

STOP

BLACK HOLE

Black holes are so heavy and have so much gravity, not even light can escape them.
There are four major types of black holes in our universe: stellar, intermediate,
miniature, and supermassive.

Although all black holes are very dense, the heaviest objects we know to exist
are supermassive black holes. These are often found at the center of galaxies.
In fact, there's a supermassive black hole at the center of our galaxy called
Sagittarius A, and it's 4 million times heavier than our sun!

But Sagittarius A isn't even the heaviest black hole known to scientists.
TON 618 was discovered in 1957
and is located more than 10
billion light-years away from Earth.
TON 618 is 242 billion miles (390
billion km) across and weighs more
than 66 billion times that of our sun.

WOW! That's 66 with nine zeros after it!

Yeah, it looks like this:

66,000,000,000

Exploring Our Solar System

Well, hello there. I am the sun. There are a few things you should know about me: I am a total star, I take up a lot of space, and I'm HOT.

In other words, I'm kind of a big deal, and the planets can't resist my gravitational pull. Just watch them spin around me! You could say I'm the STAR of the show.

Oh, and without me, there would be no life on Earth! Also, I'm real gassy and can't hold in my burps.

4.5 BILLION YEARS YOUNG

The Sun

Size: 864,000 miles (1.4 million km) wide

Hi . . . um . . . my name is Mercury, and you probably only know me by my close proximity to the sun. I'm the smallest planet in the solar system, but what I lack in size, I make up for in speed!

That's right; while it might take Earth 365 days to work its way around the sun, I zip around that big ball of gas in only 88 days! Booyah! But I spin slowly, so one day on me is 1,408 hours on Earth. (Not that I'm comparing or anything.)

Also, I basically have no atmosphere, so I'm always crazy hot during the day and freezing at night.

Oh, AND all these annoying comets and asteroids keep bumping into me, so I'm covered in giant craters. (And they're all named after famous artists, musicians, and authors, like Dr. Seuss and Walt Disney!)

And did I mention how FAST I am?

FASTEST IN THE SOLAR SYSTEM

Mercury

Hey, Earth neighbor! Venus here, hottest planet, named after the Roman goddess of love and beauty.

Venus

You may have seen me hanging out after dark. After all, I am your closest neighbor and recipient of the third-place medal for "Brightest Natural Object in the Sky."

And have I mentioned that I'm also the VOLCANO CAPITAL OF THE SOLAR SYSTEM? I'm home to over 1,600 major volcanoes.

But you'll never get to see them in person because I'm also covered in poisonous clouds and a thick atmosphere that makes me too hot to handle.

We'll just have to gaze at each other from afar. SIGH.

Hi, it's me, your planet, Earth. Listen, I know these other planets are looking pretty flashy right now, but I can assure you the grass is only greener on ME!

How do I know? Let's just say this isn't my first trip around the sun, if you know what I mean.

I've been around for 4.5 billion years—long enough to know how and when life began. And where would that be? ON ME!

Thanks to my distance from the sun, I was in the perfect spot for life to form. (That's why it's called the Goldilocks Zone! I'm JUST right.)

HOME SWEET HOME

Earth

In fact, I'm the only planet where humans have discovered life. I've got it all, baby. Water! A quirky little tilt! Fresh air! And you! Welcome home, my little life-form.

Heyo! Mars here, though some people like to call me the Red Planet. I think it's because of my color. My soil is full of this stuff called iron oxide, which is basically just rust. Anyhoo, it makes me red.

Let's see . . . I am the fourth planet from the sun; one year on me would be like 687 Earth days, so time here is not an issue; and sometimes I have really bad dust storms that can last for months.

So why would you want to visit? Well, I have the biggest mountain in the entire solar system! It's called Olympus Mons, and it's about three times the height of Mount Everest on Earth—almost 16 miles (26 km) tall!

But not everything here is big. I also have two cute little moons to keep me company. Their names are Phobos and Deimos (the smallest in the solar system).

IT MIGHT HAVE RAINED HERE ONCE

Mars

Hello. My name is Saturn. You may know me as "the jewel of the solar system." Others may know me as a big, bright, beautiful gas giant.

How giant am I? Let's just say I am NINE TIMES larger than Earth. In fact, it's possible to see me in your night sky without the help of a telescope.

But it's my rings I consider my best quality.

SATURDAY WAS NAMED AFTER ME!

Saturn

My seven icy, dusty, rocky rings span thousands of miles and dazzle the dozens of moons that orbit me.

Wow! You seem like such a sophisticated planet!

29

Hi! My name is Uranus, and for some reason, that makes people laugh. WHAT IS SO FUNNY ABOUT MY NAME?! And by the way, it's pronounced "YOOR-un-us." Go ahead, say it out loud. SAY IT! Now, stop making me the butt of all your jokes.

Anyway, the first thing you should know about me is that I smell. Real bad. Like rotten eggs mixed with toots. Don't get me confused with those gas giants over there. I'm actually an ice giant! I just happen to have all these stinky hydrogen sulfide clouds.

But don't let my smell scare you away. I've also got wind speeds that can reach 560 miles (901 km) per hour, and with a temperature of −371°F (−224°C), I can proudly declare myself the coldest planet in the solar system!

In addition, I rotate on my side like a ball rolling around the sun (and it takes me 84 Earth years to do that).

But look at my pretty blueish-green hue. My swirling clouds of methane gas MAY even rain diamonds!

IT'S PRONOUNCED YOOR-UN-US!

Uranus

What's up? I'm Neptune. I'm super far from the sun (2.8 BILLION miles/4.5 billion km) and kind of a loner out here as the most distant planet in the solar system.

And because of that, I'm dark. Very dark. It takes sunlight four hours just to get to me, and even then I'm pretty dim.

The most action you're going to get around here comes from my winds. I've got winds blowing faster than the speed of sound.

Every few years, a storm the size of Earth forms and disappears. I call it my "Great Dark Spot!"

DARK, DISTANT & STORMY

Neptune

GOING THROUGH A PHASE

Moon

GOOD NIGHT!

BLAGH! You scared me!

The moon? Where did YOU come from?

Well, some astronomers think I was formed when another planet crashed into Earth, and that I'm just a mix of all the broken pieces from the collision smashed together. But nobody knows for sure. It happened a long time ago. To be exact-ish: 4.5 billion years!

That's quite the origin story! I hope I get to walk all over you someday!

MINDY!

It's perfectly all right. I've already been walked on by 12 different astronauts. In fact, I'm the only place beyond Earth where humans have ever set foot. And I've still got the footprints to prove it!

*Earth's moon has a weak atmosphere, no air to breathe or water to drink, and really long moonquakes that can sometimes last for hours. This place is literally the pits. You should see its craters.

PLANET X!

Some scientists believe that there may be a ninth planet in our solar system, well beyond the orbit of Neptune. They call this mysterious planet Planet X! Astronomers believe that this planet would have a mass about 10 times that of Earth and orbit the sun 20 times farther away than Neptune!

Whoa! That's like 55 billion miles (88 billion Km) from the sun!

Yeah! Astronomers think it would take around 20,000 Earth years just to complete one lap!

51 PEGASI B

Ever feel like the year just drags on and on and on? Here on 51 Pegasi b that's not a problem! It only takes 102 hours to complete an orbit of its mother star, meaning a year on this planet is only four Earth days long!

ABOUT THE SAME MASS AS JUPITER

YOU'RE INVITED TO YET ANOTHER NEW YEAR'S EVE PARTY!

PROXIMA CENTAURI B

When it comes to finding a new planet, it's all about location, location, location. And Proxima Centauri b has it all!

Right in the habitable zone, only 4.2 light-years from Earth, Proxima Centauri b has a locked rotation, meaning its sun never moves in the sky. One side of the planet is in constant daylight, and the other is in constant darkness!

ABOUT THE SAME MASS AS EARTH

You mean there's a point on this planet where it's always sunset?

Yup! And a point where it's always sunrise!

KEPLER-16B

What's better than orbiting one star?
Orbiting two! And that's exactly what
you get with Kepler-16b.
That's right—two stars for the price of one!
Here on Kepler-16b you get two shadows, two sunsets,
and two sunrises each and every day.

ABOUT A THIRD OF THE MASS OF JUPITER

SALE

TRAPPIST-IE

FOR SALE

Want to add a bit of excitement to your sky? Look no further
than Trappist-1e!
Trappist-1e is one of seven planets that orbit this distant star.
But unlike our solar system, all these planets are crammed in
nice and close (all orbiting closer than Mercury does to our sun).
This means that if you were to stand on Trappist-1e and
look up to the sky, you'd see the six other planets
whipping around above your head.

Most of these
planets would
appear larger in the sky
than the **MOON** does
here on Earth!

Whoa . . .

LOCATION, LOCATION, LOCATION

When looking for a new planet, the most important thing to keep in mind is **location**.

You want a planet that's *just* right!

WELCOME TO THE GOLDILOCKS ZONE!

This is the area around a star that's not so close and hot that any liquid water on its surface could evaporate and not so far away that the water could freeze.

Still haven't found what you're looking for?

NO WORRIES!

Our team of experts will use the latest and greatest in planet-spotting technology to find you the perfect planetary home!

HOW WE'RE DOING IT!

KEPLER SPACE TELESCOPE

The Kepler Space Telescope was launched into orbit around Earth in 2009. Since then it's discovered more than 2,662 exoplanets!

More than half of all discovered exoplanets have been found using the Kepler Telescope.

THAT ONE LOOKS COZY!

JAMES WEBB SPACE TELESCOPE

Launched in 2022, the James Webb Space Telescope is the largest, most powerful, and most advanced telescope ever created. It's currently pointed toward the deep reaches of space, searching for your perfect planet.

So when are we leaving, Guy Raz?!

Well, Mindy, although we've discovered more than 4,000 exoplanets outside our solar system . . .

BONKERBALLS!

Most aren't likely capable of hosting human life.

But many astronomers think it's only a matter of time before we find what they refer to as an Earth twin.

I'm *seeing* double here!

ANIMALS IN SPACE

Mindy, I had no idea so many animals had been to space!

Oh yeah, it's a real jungle up there!

Let's take a look at some of these groundbreaking animal astronauts!

The Great Hall of Animal Astronauts

When you consider space travel's greatest successes, you might think of Soviet cosmonaut Yuri Gagarin's first trip into space or Neil Armstrong's first steps on the moon. But humans aren't the only ones setting records!

FRUIT FLY:
FIRST LIVING ANIMAL IN SPACE

The fruit fly was the first animal to make it to space! These brave insects were transported to the edge of space on the back of a V-2 rocket on February 20, 1947. They were part of a mission to study the effect of cosmic radiation on organic matter.

Cosmic radiation is a type of energy that is everywhere in outer space. Back in 1947, scientists really didn't know how this energy would affect living things.

When it comes to genetics, it turns out that humans and fruit flies have more in common than you might think. In fact, we share 60 percent of the same DNA! This research came in handy when human beings were sent up into space 14 years later.

The edge of space, according to NASA, is about 60 miles (100 km) above sea level. These fruit flies made it 68 miles (109 km) above Earth, meaning they only *just* made it to space.

DNA is the genetic information inside the cells of the body that helps to make all living things who they are.

Laika, the first dog in space, had a real rags-to-riches story. She was a homeless dog that first underwent a series of tests to make sure she was the right pup for the job. (Soviet scientists thought homeless dogs could better withstand the cold of the spaceship.)

Laika was able to make four orbits of the earth in Sputnik 2, which launched into space on November 3, 1957.

LAIKA THE DOG:
FIRST ANIMAL TO MAKE AN ORBITAL FLIGHT IN A SPACECRAFT

HAM THE CHIMP:
FIRST APE IN SPACE

HAIL TO THE CHIMP!

Great apes such as chimpanzees, orangutans, and humans are some of the smartest animals on the planet. We humans might like to think that we're the brainiest of the bunch, but we didn't get to space first!

Ham the chimpanzee was sent into space on January 31, 1961, three whole months before Yuri Gagarin, the first human in space, and four months before Alan Shepard, the first American in space!

DID YOU KNOW?

In 2015, researchers sent a group of flatworms to the International Space Station to see how they would fare after five weeks in space. What they found was totally BONKERBALLS! Not only did some of these flatworms spontaneously divide in two, but in one case, the two halves each grew back TWO HEADS!

TORTOISE A AND TORTOISE B:
FIRST ANIMALS TO ORBIT THE MOON

One small waddle for a tortoise.
One giant plunge for tortoise-kind!

On July 16, 1969, Neil Armstrong became the first person to set foot on the moon. A half year before that, in December 1968, astronauts Frank Borman, Jim Lovell, and Bill Anders became the first people to orbit the moon.

But before humans orbited the moon, two Soviet tortoises aboard the Zond 5 spacecraft became the first living creatures to ever make it to the moon and back on September 15, 1968.

And an orbit is a path that an object . . .

Like a spacecraft . . .

Like the moon!

Makes around another object in space . . .

HOPE THE COCKROACH:
FIRST ANIMAL TO GIVE BIRTH IN SPACE (SPACE MOM)

In 2007, aboard a Soviet Foton-M satellite, a cockroach named Hope became the first creature to give birth in space. She became the proud mom of 33 adorable little space cockroach babies!

And that's not all! Here's a list of some other animal earthlings that have spent time in space:

Mice!
Rats! Rabbits!
Cats! Spiders! Worms!
Ants! Bees! Newts!
Geckos! Fish! Jellyfish!
Frogs! Guinea Pigs!
Tardigrades!

Tardigrade Tough

In 2007, microscopic invertebrates called tardigrades proved once and for all that they might be the toughest creatures on Earth. Not only can they live for up to 30 years without water, but they can also survive the harsh conditions of space without any protection at all! This was discovered when the European Space Agency put a bunch of them outside of the spaceship for 12 days. When they brought them back to Earth, they discovered that most of the tardigrades had survived!

STARS

A STAR is BORN

When you look up at a night sky full of stars, it might seem like they've been there—and will be there—forever. But just like everything else in the universe, stars go through their own unique and fascinating life cycle!

Look at all these newborn stars, Guy Raz! They're so cute I'm gonna barf!

It really gives new meaning to the words A STAR IS BORN!

★ The most stars you could possibly see on a night sky is around 2,500.

PROTOSTAR

Stars begin as giant clouds of dust and gas called nebulae. Over time, gravity causes the dust and gas to bunch up, becoming hotter and hotter until they become a protostar.

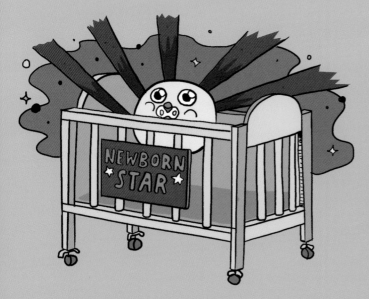

Once that protostar gets hot enough, something called nuclear fusion happens, and a young star is born!

This phase of life lasts approximately 100,000 to 10 million years, depending on the size of the star.

Nuclear fusion happens when hydrogen is converted into helium. This expels a huge amount of energy, resulting in *a lot* of **heat** and *a lot* of **light!**

MAIN SEQUENCE STAR

Once nuclear fusion is achieved, stars can continue to burn energy and glow for billions of years.

Stars will spend most of their lives in this stage. Once the star runs out of fuel (hydrogen), it moves into the next part of life.

RED GIANT

Once a star has run out of hydrogen to convert into helium, it starts to expand. During this phase, it can grow to more than 100 times its original size.

Over the next few hundred million years, the star will start to use helium to power itself. In other words, it EATS ITSELF! Once the star has run out of helium, it begins the final stage of its life cycle.

COLLAPSE

After nibbling through all its helium, the star will start to make carbon in its core. This causes the star to shrink and collapse upon itself. What happens next depends on its size.

★ The red giant could become a new kind of star called a white dwarf. These are much smaller than any other kind of star and have no energy left. The immense heat produced when they collapse causes them to keep on shining. Scientists have predicted that it could take hundreds of billions of years for these stars to cool off. But since the universe is only 13.8 billion years old, nobody knows how long this stage of the life cycle will last!

★ If the star is particularly large (five or more times larger than our sun), it won't become a white dwarf. Instead, its collapse will result in a huge explosion known as a supernova!

Supernovas are some of the largest and most violent events in the cosmos. Once the dust has settled, they usually result in the creation of either a neutron star or a black hole!

That's some light show!

Wow!

Our sun is our closest star. The next closest is Proxima Centauri, which is 4.246 light-years away.

FAMOUS STARS

> And if you look to your left, you'll see some of the most interesting stars in the universe!

> Oooooooooh!

There may be as many as 400 billion stars in our galaxy alone!

BINARY STARS

Like two peas in a pod, binary stars are always there for each other!

Binary stars are two stars whose gravity forces are so equally matched that they start to orbit each other. They are known as companion stars.

> I'm the brighter star, so they call me the Primary Star!

> And they call me the Secondary Star!

SAO 206462

A STAR WITH SPIRAL ARMS

SAO 206462 is located about 460 light-years from Earth. Its "spiral arms" are wrapped around itself, as if it's giving itself a big hug! The arms are made of gas and dust, and they extend about twice as far as Pluto's orbit around our sun.

Astronomers think this is evidence of early planet formation. Baby planets could be curled up in those arms!

Over the next several million years, these dust and gases will clump together to create planets.

Has a nice ring to it!

BILLION YEARS

Let's check back on this star in a few million years, Guy Raz.

STAR SAO 206462

Good idea! By then this star might have its very own solar system!

Stars can come in RED, WHITE, and BLUE. ★

LUCY

THE DIAMOND STAR

Lucy is a star in the constellation of Centaurus that has a sparkly little secret in its core. The star is super dense: it's only as big as the moon, but it weighs as much as the sun.

Like the Beatles song!

Lucy is also surprisingly *cool*, only reaching a temperature of 10,832°F (6,000°C). In comparison, our sun has an average temperature of 27,000,000°F (15,000,000°)C!

By looking at how Lucy pulsates from bright to dim, scientists were able to determine that its carbon core has crystallized to form a diamond 10 billion trillion trillion carats in size!

★ Scientists have predicted that there are around 200 billion trillion (200,000,000,000,000,000,000,000) stars in the known universe.

★ Stars don't actually twinkle. The shimmering you see is caused when the light from those stars passes through our atmosphere and interacts with its gases.

THE SQUASHED STAR

Well known to astronomers, Vega is only visible from the northern hemisphere.

VEGA

Although it looks round to us on Earth, if we examined it from another angle, we'd see that Vega is actually squashed flat like a pancake! That's because of its high spin rate, or how fast it takes to complete one rotation. (Earth takes 24 hours to complete one rotation.)

Vega may be twice the size of our sun, but it's way faster! Vega completes one rotation in just 12.5 hours. (Our sun takes 27 *days* to spin around!)

These high speeds force the mass at Vega's equator to be pushed out, like a person holding onto a merry-go-round as it spins.

Here on Earth, we view Vega from the top down, so it looks perfectly round, but if we were to view it from the side we'd see that it is in fact very, very squished!

Hold on tight, Guy Raz!

AGGHHHHH!

Back in my day, we had to make do with just TWO periodic elements . . . and we didn't complain about it, either!

HD 140283

This star is named after the oldest man in the Bible.

THE STAR THAT'S BEEN THERE FROM THE BEGINNING!

Methuselah is a subgiant star located just 190 light-years from Earth. Astronomers first estimated that it was 16 billion years old—2.2 billion years older than the universe itself! Upon further research, though, they realized that number is actually 13.7 billion. That means this star must have been formed in the first few million years after the big bang.

By studying Methuselah, scientists are hoping to learn more about how early stars and galaxies formed after the big bang.

If you tried to hitch a ride on the fastest spacecraft ever launched, it would still take you more than 70,000 years to reach our closest neighboring star, Proxima Centauri.

STAR SPOTTERS' GUIDE

AND THIS TRADITION OF STAR SPOTTING IS STILL ALIVE AND WELL TODAY! IN FACT, IT'S SOMETHING YOU CAN DO YOURSELF THANKS TO THIS SUPEREXCLUSIVE STAR SPOTTING GUIDE!

There are tons of stars (and planets) that you should be able to see from your own backyard using only your bare eyeballs! Keep an eye out for these:

But better be quick; Venus only hangs around for a short time after the sun has set. It reappears just before dawn, which is how it got the nickname the Morning Star.

Sirius

Sirius is the brightest star in the night sky. It's highly visible in the northern hemisphere, particularly on a clear winter night. To find it, look for a very bright star with a blueish-white tinge to it. It shimmers with other colors if you catch it low in the sky—that's why it's sometimes called a rainbow star!

Betelgeuse

This reddish-looking star is named after the Arabic words *bat al-jawz ā*, which mean "the giant's shoulder." Betelgeuse can be seen by first finding Sirius, then looking down toward the horizon.

CONSTELLATIONS

Sometimes we make shapes and pictures out of groups of stars. These are called constellations.

HYDRA

The largest constellation in the night sky, hydra is meant to represent a sea serpent.

HERCULES

A constellation named after the Roman mythological hero Hercules.

ORION

One of the most well-known constellations on Earth, visible from just about anywhere! It is named after Orion, a hunter in Greek mythology.

Some constellations can only be seen from certain places on Earth, such as the northern hemisphere. Here are just a few examples:

NORTHERN HEMISPHERE EXCLUSIVE!

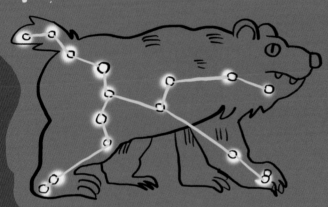

URSA MAJOR

Also called the Great Bear, Ursa Major is well known for containing the Big Dipper!

SOUTHERN HEMISPHERE EXCLUSIVE!

CRUX

More commonly known as the Southern Cross, this constellation is only viewable in the southern hemisphere and appears on five national flags: New Zealand, Australia, Brazil, Samoa, and Papua New Guinea.

Black Holes

SINGULARITY

The very center of a black hole. It can weigh anywhere from a few times as heavy as our sun to thousands of millions of times heavier than our sun. And all of this is squeezed into a space no larger than a pinhead!

It's this incredible density that gives black holes their extreme gravitational pull. The pull is so strong that nothing can escape it, not even light. That's why they're practically invisible!

Whoa, what do you think's in there?

Don't get too close, Mindy! You'll get sucked in!

EVENT HORIZON

Once you cross this line, there's no way for you to escape the gravitational pull of a black hole. It doesn't matter if you're a photon, a spaceship, or a cloud of dirt and gas; once you reach the event horizon—*SLURP*—you're getting slurped up!

ACCRETION DISK

This big, swirling ring surrounds an event horizon. It's created by stars and other space dust that's sucked into a black hole. As the stars get closer to an event horizon, they spin around the black hole's center, like water swirling down a drain. And as each star is ripped apart, its remaining gas moves faster and faster around the center. It heats up and creates an intensely bright ring called a quasar.

RELATIVISTIC JET

Black holes are messy eaters! Once they've finished gobbling up a star, they sometimes burp excess radiation and particles back out into space. These burps often travel at incredible speeds, sometimes even approaching the speed of light.

Help! Pasta rope!!

SPAGHETTIFICATION

Gravity increases the closer you get to a black hole. For example, if you were to jump into it feetfirst, the pull on the bottom part of your body would be stronger than the pull on the top, STREEEEETCHING you out like a big ol' noodle!

Know Your Black Holes

STELLAR

Stellar black holes are the most common type of black hole in our universe and can weigh up to 24 times as much as our sun.

INTERMEDIATE

Intermediate black holes are rare. They are often formed when two or more stellar black holes merge together and can weigh 100 to 1,000 times more than our sun!

Not too small, not too big—this black hole is JUST right!

Supermassive

Supermassive black holes are . . . well, supermassive! They typically lurk at the center of galaxies and can weigh millions or even billions of times more than our sun!

How Is a Black Hole Formed?

After a big star, like a red giant, has run out of gas, it rapidly contracts and collapses upon itself, resulting in a . . .

SUPERNOVA!

Supernovas are a star's last big hoorah—a massive explosion that leaves behind a dense core.

If the star is large enough (typically 20 times as heavy as our sun), once the dust from the supernova has settled, it will develop into either a neutron star or, if *very* heavy . . . a black hole!

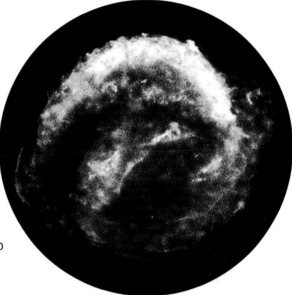

Time moves slower the closer you get to a black hole!

It might seem like science fiction, but there's actually a way to travel *forward* in time! If you were somehow able to resist the gravitational pull of a black hole and walk toward it, time would move more slowly the closer you came to the event horizon. What might have only felt like an hour-long space walk to you would have taken years for the rest of the crew on your spaceship! This is because black holes have such intense gravity that they warp both space and time around them.

Stargazing Gadgets

Stargazing—it's not just for camping!

Throughout history, humans have used the stars to help navigate the high seas and learn more about our planetary neighbors and the origins of our universe.

Mindy! I think this one might be broken.

You're using it upside down, Guy Raz!

Whoops!

The Sextant

HELPING YOU GO WHERE YOU GOTTA GO!

LOST AT SEA WITH NO GPS? NO PROBLEM!

INTRODUCING THE SEXTANT!

Trusted since the early 1700s, the sextant has been used by sailors and navigators to help find their way when lost at sea.

TIMELESS

Sextants are still used by some seafarers today!

BUT HOW DOES IT WORK?

The sextant uses state-of-the-art optical science by lining up one of the device's mirrors with a light source—such as the sun or a bright star—and the other with the horizon. This way, you can accurately determine exactly where you are on the globe!

FUN FACT!

The word **sextant** comes from the Latin word for six: *sextus*. This is because the sextant can be rotated 60 degrees, or 1/6 of a complete circle.

THE TELESCOPE

Get up close & personal... to the STARS!

CAROLINE HERSCHEL

Our expertly crafted telescopes work by having a combination of two lenses, which are curved pieces of glass.

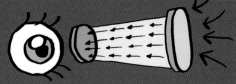

THE MAN HIMSELF

First invented by world renowned scientist and craftsman Galileo Galilei in 1609, the telescope is one of our best sellers!

Did you know he also invented the pendulum clock?

Hey! I know that guy!

THE OBJECTIVE LENS

This the light coming in from whatever star, planet, or celestial object you're trying to observe and focuses it into a very fine point within the telescope.

THE EYEPIECE LENS

This works as a sort of magnifying glass that expands the fine point of light created by the objective lens into something we can see!

YOUR EYES!

One of the best-known gadgets for stargazing is located right on your face: your eyes! Humans have been looking up at the stars for thousands of years. The most important thing for successfully viewing stars with your eyes is to find somewhere dark!

I guess you could say we're experienced star snoopers.

I'm even wearing star-snooping spectacles!

LIGHT POLLUTION

This is the glow in the night sky created by artificial, human-made light. It's often created by buildings and streetlights and is so powerful that it obscures the light from stars in the night sky.

DARK SKY ZONES

These are areas around the world that are often far away from cities, towns, and other sources of artificial light. This means that they are not as affected by light pollution and make it easier to spot stars.

Darkest Place on Earth!

According to a study in 2021, the Roque de los Muchachos Observatory in the Canary Islands is the darkest place on Earth—making it the perfect place for a spot of stargazing.

SPACE ROCKS!

ASTEROIDS & COMETS & METEORS

Oh my!

There are lots of different space rocks floating around up there! But not all are created equal. Most are split up into three separate categories.

ASTEROIDS

Asteroids make up the vast majority of space rocks floating around our solar system. There are about a million of them in the asteroid belt between Mars and Jupiter.

Asteroids are typically made out of rocks and metals and come in all shapes and sizes, ranging from 33 feet (10 m) to more than 300 miles (483 km) in diameter.

The asteroid that slammed into Earth about 65 million years ago, resulting in the dinosaurs' extinction, was only about 6 miles (10 km) in diameter. That's about the size of 26 Empire State Buildings stacked on top of one another.

COMETS

I'm blazing my own trail!

Comets are like asteroids except they are typically made of ice! Comets also tend to travel alone and have unique (and often lopsided) orbits around the sun. When a comet approaches the sun, it heats up and starts to melt. The gas that's created forms a long tail that trails behind it. This tail can sometimes look like streaks of hair. In fact, the word comet comes from the Greek word *kométēs*, meaning "having long hair."

METEOROIDS

A meteoroid is just like an asteroid, only smaller! Meteoroids range in size from a grain of rice to a large boulder.

It's like a little baby asteroid!

METEORS

Meteors are meteoroids that get sucked in by Earth's gravity. Friction causes them to heat up and glow as they pass through our atmosphere before ultimately burning out.

Wait a minute, Mindy, are we talking about shooting stars?

Yup! That's all meteors are— shooting stars!

METEOR SHOWERS

Meteor showers happen when several meteoroids pass through our atmosphere at the same time. This usually occurs when Earth passes through a cluster of meteoroids on its path around the sun.

Like passing through a swarm of mosquitoes on a road trip!

Turn on the wipers, Mindy!

SPLAT

WOW

DID YOU KNOW?

Something sudden, brilliant, and swift is often referred to as METEORIC.

Like an actor's meteoric rise to fame!

METEORITES

A meteorite is a meteoroid that *doesn't* burn up in Earth's atmosphere. Instead, it makes impact with Earth's surface! This is very rare.

DID YOU KNOW?

On June 30, 1908, just above the Tunguska River in central Siberia, a meteorite flattened about 772 square miles (2,000 square km) of trees. That's half the size of Rhode Island!

GOLD RUSH

Are you looking to make a quick buck? Check out the asteroid 16 Psyche. Located between Mars and Jupiter, 16 Psyche is made up almost entirely of gold!

In fact, there's enough gold* on 16 Psyche to make everyone on Earth a billionaire multiple times over. Experts have estimated that the different metals on this asteroid are worth more than $10,000 quadrillion.

*Asteroid 16 Psyche may not actually be made of gold. It may be made up of nickel or iron. More information available after NASA mission in 2026. Invest at your own risk.

ASTEROID BELTS AND WHERE TO FIND THEM

Trojan Asteroids

There are two large clusters of asteroids that follow the same path around the sun as Jupiter. One cluster is just in front of Jupiter and the other is just behind it.

Inner Asteroid Belt

The majority of the asteroids in our solar system are found here, between the orbits of Mars and Jupiter.

Kuiper Belt

The Kuiper Belt is a string of asteroids found beyond the orbit of Neptune. Most of these are thought to be made of ice!

MOON! Planets always orbit around a star, sucked in by their strong gravitational pull. However, many smaller objects often get sucked into planets' gravitational pull, too. When this happens (and they orbit around that planet), they become moons. Here on Earth we only have one moon, but some planets have as many as 82!

ASTEROIDS! Asteroids, like planets, also orbit stars! But unlike planets, asteroids come in all shapes and sizes. Planets are often so big and dense that gravity itself squeezes them into round, spherical shapes. If you're not round and spherical, then you may be too small to be considered a planet.

DEMOTED!

Pluto was once considered the ninth planet in our solar system, but in 2006, it was demoted to a dwarf planet because it didn't fulfill the third criteria for becoming a planet.

DWARF PLANET! So, you:
1. Orbit the sun
2. Are round and spherical

But there are a bunch of other objects, like asteroids or other dwarf planets, crowding your space.

Dwarf planets are objects that are large enough to be squeezed into a spherical shape (bigger than an asteroid), but not large enough to clear other objects from their orbit (smaller than a regular planet).

PLANET! Congratulations! You've passed the three tests of becoming a planet!
1. Orbits a Star
2. Spherical or Round
3. Has cleared other objects in its orbit.

You'll be joining a very elite class of celestial objects, with eight other planets in our solar system alone!

ALIEN LIFE (?)

Don't worry, Guy Raz! It's just us!

AAH!

So much for the search for intelligent life!

FOR SALE

AWESOME ALIENS!

SMOOTH GRAY SKIN

When you think of aliens, you probably think of something like this:

BIG BUGGY EYES!

SIGNIFICANT LACK OF NOSE

But some scientists believe that our first contact with an extraterrestrial species will be microbial!

Microbial?

Yes! Tiny living organisms like bacteria and fungi!

Extraterrestrial refers to any object or being that is not from Earth. It comes from the Latin words for "beyond" and "Earth."

IS THERE LIFE ON MARS?

The search for extraterrestrial life has already begun on Mars. NASA's Perseverance rover landed on the red planet in February 2021 and has been searching for signs of ancient life ever since.

   Perseverance has been examining an area known as Jezero Crater. It's an ancient lake bed that may have once contained microbial life.

GUY ⭐

⭐ MINDY

WE'LL FIND THE RIGHT PLANET FOR YOU!

Not feeling Mars? No problem! There are plenty of places in our solar system where microbes could feel right at home:

FOR SALE

VENUS

ONE OF THE MAJOR PLANETS IN OUR SOLAR SYSTEM

AVERAGE TEMPERATURE: 867°F (464°C)

Venus is often referred to as Earth's twin because the two are so similar in size and shape. Scientists believe Venus was once covered in water, but thanks to a runaway greenhouse effect, it's now all dried up! Some think that certain chemicals in Venus's atmosphere could have been created by living organisms!

CLOSE ENCOUNTERS DEBUNKED!

Join the detectives Mindy Thomas and Guy Raz as they debunk the greatest interstellar mysteries of all time!

THE PYRAMIDS

The Myth: The Great Pyramids of Giza in Egypt were created so long ago and are so complicated that ancient humans must have had extra-terrestrial help, right?

Pass me the wrench!

The Truth: Just because people lived a long time ago doesn't mean they weren't capable of creating great, towering pyramids! In fact, there have been several archaeological finds that explain the techniques and tools ancient Egyptians used to create these massive stone tombs!

AREA 51

The Myth: Area 51 is a secret military base that the US government uses to hide the existence of extraterrestrials. In 1947, one of these aliens escaped in a flying saucer before crash landing in a nearby town called Roswell, in New Mexico.

The Truth: Although there is a military base that is popularly (but not officially) referred to as Area 51, there is no evidence it's home to intergalactic visitors. The "flying saucer" that crashed in Roswell in 1947 was, in fact, from the military base, but it wasn't an alien spacecraft. It was a weather balloon that the military was developing to spy on enemies.

CROP CIRCLES

The Myth: Proof of aliens visiting Earth can be found in crop fields all over the world. Crop circles are large circular patterns that seemingly appear out of nowhere overnight. Must be calling cards from alien visitors, right?

The Truth: Wrong! The mystery of crop circles was officially solved in 1987, when a man by the name of Dave Chorley confessed to creating hundreds of these patterns all over England in the 1970s and 1980s. Most crop circles found outside of England have been attributed to copycat artists!

THE SEARCH CONTINUES...

For thousands of years, humans have looked up at the stars and wondered if anyone else was looking back.

Today, there is one organization trying to answer that age-old question: Is there intelligent life in the universe?

INTRODUCING SETI!

SETI is a nonprofit organization that was founded in 1984. The scientists and astronomers at SETI use giant radio telescopes to analyze radio waves from space. They do this to try to determine whether any of the signals could have been created by an intelligent alien species.

I wonder . . .

SEARCH FOR

EXTRA

TERRESTRIAL

INTELLIGENCE

Kind of like scrolling through static on your car radio, trying to pick up a signal.

Exactly!

Hey there, Earthlings! Flip and Mozi here, live from K-WOW Galactic!

KRSHHHHT

We've also been sending our own specialized radio signals into space for almost 50 years, a sort of welcome message for any aliens that might be doing the same thing!

Each radio and television signal transmitted on Earth also makes its way into space!

Every broadcast we've ever made is currently making its way across the galaxy at almost the speed of light! This means that an alien species' first introduction to humans may be an old episode of a TV show!

Ugh! Another rerun!

I DO love Lucy!

DOING THE MATH

What are the odds of there being alien life in outer space? Well, believe it or not, someone's already done the math!

$$N = R_* f_p n_e f_l f_i f_c L.$$

The Drake equation was first thought up by astronomer Frank Drake in 1961 as a way to calculate how many alien civilizations might exist that are capable of communicating with us. Although this equation is extremely difficult to calculate, astronomers were able to estimate that there could be anywhere from 1,000 to 100 million planets with alien civilizations in our galaxy alone!

SPACE ODDITIES

LOST & FOUND

If there's one thing humans love to do, it's leave their stuff everywhere! Here are some things humans have left on the surface of the moon.

A **hammer** and a **feather**: These were part of a science experiment to demonstrate how gravity works on the moon. (If both were dropped at once, can you guess which one hit the moon's surface first? Hint: it's a trick question!)

Two **golf balls**: Astronaut Alan Shepard hit these across the surface of the moon and never returned to pick them up.

A family **photo**: A signed photo of astronaut Charles Duke's family now sits on the moon.

A gold replica of an **olive branch**: a symbol of peace.

Footprints: In 1969, when Neil Armstrong became the first human to set foot on the moon, he created some pretty famous footprints. And with no wind, rain, or weather up there, those footprints are still around today.

The **Bible**

12 pairs of **space boots**: The astronauts on Apollo 11 needed to lighten their load before heading back to Earth, so they left their boots on the moon.

A **TV camera**: Neil Armstrong and Buzz Aldrin used a TV camera to film the first moon landing. When they finished recording, they decided to leave the camera there.

Three **lunar rovers**

A commemorative **plaque** from the Apollo 11 mission: "Here men from the planet Earth first set foot upon the moon. July 1969 A.D. We came in peace for all mankind."

One tiny **silicon disc**: this is inscribed with tiny messages from the leaders of 73 countries.

96 **bags** of astronauts' pee and poop

A whole bunch of **US flags**

HERE MEN FROM THE PLANET EARTH FIRST SET FOOT UPON THE MOON JULY 1969 AD WE CAME IN PEACE

Ashes: American geologist Gene Shoemaker discovered so many comets and planets that NASA (and his family) decided to leave his ashes on the moon after he died.

Two **medals** and a 3.5-inch (9-cm) tall aluminum **sculpture** called *Fallen Astronaut*: these were left to honor American astronauts and Soviet cosmonauts who died during space missions or training exercises.

Part of the **Eagle lunar module**: Part of the module that Neil Armstrong and Buzz Aldrin used to travel from the Apollo 11 space rocket to the surface of the moon and back.

SPACE EXPLORATION

the past, PRESENT & FUTURE OF ROCKET SHIPS

Gravity is what keeps us and everything around us planted here on Earth. Escaping gravitational pull takes *a lot* of energy!

So where can we find the energy to escape Earth's gravitational pull?

One word, Guy Raz: ROCKETS!

TIMELINE OF ROCKETEERING'S GREATEST HITS!

1232: Fire Arrows

The first recorded use of rockets came from ancient China. In CE 1232, they started using explosive gunpowder to launch arrows at enemy soldiers during battle!

FZZZT

Robert Goddard is considered by many to be the father of modern rocketry. The largest spaceflight center in the world, in Greenbelt, Maryland, is named after him.

1926: Robert Goddard and His Liquid-Fueled Rocket

In March 1926, Robert Goddard successfully launched the world's first liquid-powered rocket. This would lay the foundation for all space-faring rockets to come.

1957: Sputnik

The 8K71PS rocket, otherwise known as the Sputnik launch vehicle, was the first rocket that looked like . . . well, a rocket. It was developed by Sergei Korolev, a Soviet scientist, in the early 1950s. On October 4, 1957, Sputnik was used to perform the world's first ever satellite launch.

1967: Saturn V

The Saturn V is the most iconic rocket of all time! Despite being more than 50 years old, it's still the only rocket to transport humans outside of Earth's orbit. (It was used for all nine moon missions!)

It's also the most powerful rocket ever created, capable of carrying around 260,000 pounds (118,000 kg) of cargo into space! It holds the record for the most expensive rocket program of all time, costing NASA $6.417 billion.

That's about $50 billion in today's money!

Imagine how many Tart Pops you could buy with that kind of dough!

That's one good-looking rocket!

And they were reusable!

Technically, Mindy, it's a reusable, low Earth orbital spacecraft.

1981: Space Shuttle

The space shuttle was used from 1981 until 2011 to transport cargo and astronauts between Earth and the International Space Station. During this 30-year period, more than 130 missions were completed!

Today: SpaceX Falcon 9

Today, most cargo is ferried to the International Space Station in a rocket called the Falcon 9, which was developed by a private company called SpaceX. Like the space shuttle, the Falcon 9 is reusable. Once it returns to Earth, it can simply be restocked and sent back to the ISS.

Reduce, reuse, recycle!

Rockets, that is!

2024: Orion Spacecraft

The latest and greatest in rocket science and space travel is the Orion spacecraft. A company called Lockheed Martin is building this human spacecraft for a series of NASA deep-space missions that will take place over the next several decades.

HOW A SPACE SHUTTLE WORKS

Takeoff

The space shuttle takes off from Kennedy Space Center in Cape Canaveral, Florida

Detaching

At a height of 150,000 feet (45,720 meters), the rocket boosters detach from the shuttle, parachuting down safely into the ocean.

POP

POP

Orbit

Once in orbit, the shuttle hangs out for anywhere from a couple of days to two weeks. The longest mission saw the space shuttle Columbia stay in orbit for 17 days and 15 hours.

Reentry

When it's time to come back to Earth, the shuttle reenters the atmosphere at a speed of around 17,500 miles (28,164 km) per hour. It then deploys its speed brakes and starts to slow down.

Landing

Safely back in Earth's atmosphere and moving at a reasonable speed, the shuttle then glides and lands, similarly to a plane, on a specially built runway on Merritt Island in Florida.

Ready to be launched into space again!

Like I said: REUSABLE!

There are only **58 years** between the Wright brothers' first successful airplane flight in 1903 (traveling 4 miles/6 km) and Yuri Gagarin's first successful spaceflight in 1961 (completing a lap around the entire planet)!

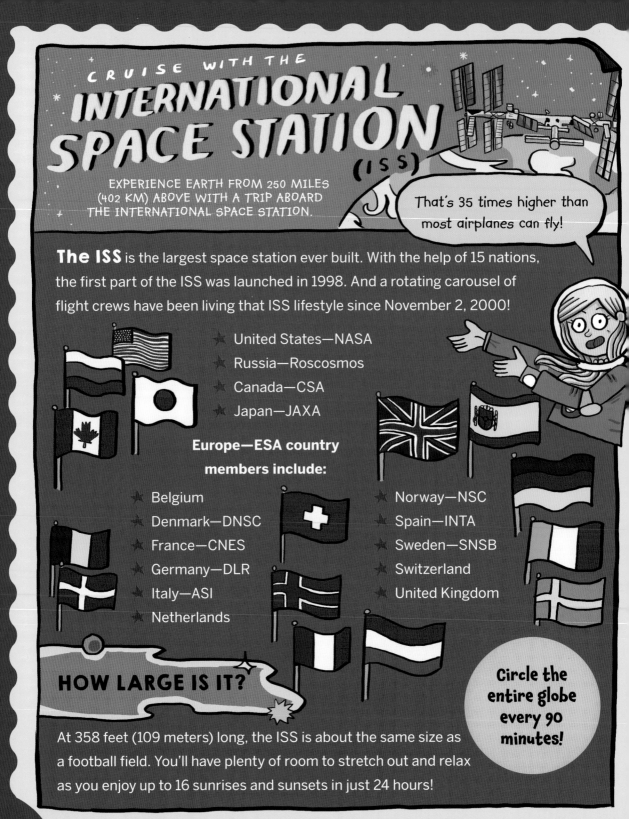

INTERNATIONAL SPACE STATION (ISS)

EXPERIENCE EARTH FROM 250 MILES (402 KM) ABOVE WITH A TRIP ABOARD THE INTERNATIONAL SPACE STATION.

That's 35 times higher than most airplanes can fly!

The ISS is the largest space station ever built. With the help of 15 nations, the first part of the ISS was launched in 1998. And a rotating carousel of flight crews have been living that ISS lifestyle since November 2, 2000!

United States—NASA
Russia—Roscosmos
Canada—CSA
Japan—JAXA

Europe—ESA country members include:

Belgium
Denmark—DNSC
France—CNES
Germany—DLR
Italy—ASI
Netherlands

Norway—NSC
Spain—INTA
Sweden—SNSB
Switzerland
United Kingdom

HOW LARGE IS IT?

Circle the entire globe every 90 minutes!

At 358 feet (109 meters) long, the ISS is about the same size as a football field. You'll have plenty of room to stretch out and relax as you enjoy up to 16 sunrises and sunsets in just 24 hours!

Got a *Need* for *Speed*?

Say goodbye to the 65 miles (105 km) speed per hour limits on Earth. The ISS whizzes around at top speeds of 17,500 miles (28,164 km) per hour. That's 5 miles (8 km) per *second*!

ALL-INCLUSIVE!*

★ Enjoy three packaged meals a day from a robust menu of over 200 food and beverage options!

★ Choose between the ISS's six crew cabin sleeping facilities.

★ Relieve yourself in either of the ISS's two vacuum-powered toilets!

★ WHAT IN THE WOW?! NASA spent $23 million to update space toilets and sent one to the ISS in 2020!

★ Check out our state-of-the-art, multipurpose gym!

VHOOMP

*Space walks not included.

Just put it on the plastic!

PRICING:
Just $55,000,000 for a luxurious, seven-night stay!*

*Prices may vary.

In 2021, a crew of private astronauts paid about $55 million each to stay on the ISS for eight days! Private flights to the ISS can cost *at least* $50 million for a weeklong stay.

103

GALAXY GEAR

Stepping out into space is serious business. Just as you wouldn't scuba dive without scuba gear, you wouldn't want to travel to space without being prepared for the harsh conditions!

The good news is that scientists and engineers have been working for over 50 years to perfect the ultimate space gear for both comfort and safety. Let's take a look!

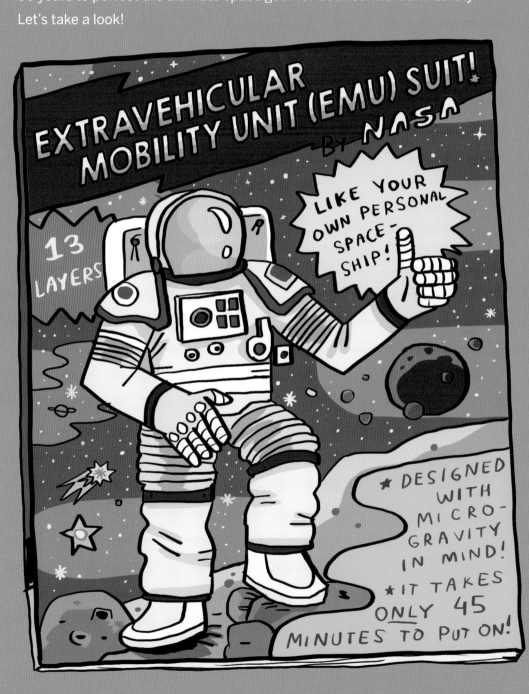

YOUR BODY IN SPACE

So you want to go to space? Well, space travel—while an out-of-this-world, bonkerballs experience—can have some strange effects on the body. Before you go, here is what you should know.

YOU MAY EXPERIENCE:

SPACE SICKNESS

When you arrive, you may have headaches, sleepiness, and nausea. These symptoms are known as Space Adaptation Syndrome. It's completely normal and should only last a few days.

Hey, I'm 6 foot 2!

Maybe on the MOON you are!

A TEMPORARY GROWTH SPURT

In space, your body could grow an extra 2 inches (5 cm) taller! Without Earth's gravity pulling your bones and spine closer together, your body is able to stretch to its full potential. But it won't last forever. When you return to Earth, you can expect to shrink down to your normal size.

FEELING LIKE YOU HAVE TO PEE ALL THE TIME

It's important for astronauts to use the bathroom *one more time* before liftoff. This is because when you arrive in space, your bodily fluids start to build up in certain areas, tricking your body into thinking it's carrying too much water. Your body responds by making more pee!

A BIG, PUFFY HEAD

On Earth, gravity helps pull our bodily fluids down to our lower half. In space, those fluids are free to flow to the upper half . . . even the head. So don't be surprised if you look in the mirror and see a big, puffy face. Like most things in space, this is only temporary.

WONKY VISION

In space, it's possible for your head to get so puffy that it actually changes the shape of your eyeballs and optic nerves. Because of this, you may find your sense of sight going a little wonky. But don't worry; your vision should go back to normal within a few years.

PUNY MUSCLES

In space, it's difficult to maintain muscle mass. With very little gravity, your muscles are out of a job! Actions like moving your body, getting your heart pumping, and moving blood throughout your vessels are pretty effortless. Sounds good, right? Not so much. This lack of effort can cause your muscles to weaken, especially during a long mission. That's why it's important for astronauts to get about two hours of exercise every day!

SLEEPLESS NIGHTS! AND SLEEPLESS DAYS!

Astronauts who have spent a lot of time in space have reported that it's hard to sleep up there. No one for sure knows why, but some scientists suspect it might have to do with the large number of sunrises and sunsets. The body doesn't know when it's night and when it's day. In other words, 24 hours up there doesn't feel the same as down here.

NO MORE SNORING

Say goodbye to snoring! When you're in microgravity, it's easier for air to pass through your nose, mouth, and throat. This makes it hard to get your snore on in space.

That's it! I want my money back.

LOST FINGERNAILS

You may want to think twice before getting a manicure before a space mission. The pressurized air from your spacesuit will stiffen the rubber linings of your gloves, making them feel like bike tires. After a while, the friction and pressure on your fingertips can cause your fingernails to fall off. This is so common, it even has a name: DELAMINATION.

Say goodbye to your fingernails!

Say hello to delamination!

Ew.

THINGS WE HAVE BECAUSE OF
SPACE TRAVEL RESEARCH

Research conducted for space travel and exploration has brought some incredible inventions that we use every day here on Earth! Here are just a few of those inventions. How many have you used?

ARTIFICIAL LIMBS

Innovations originally designed for space vehicles, like robotic arms, have led to more comfortable and lifelike artificial limbs for humans.

SCRATCH-RESISTANT LENSES

The scratch-resistant technology used in eyeglasses was first developed by NASA for the visors of space helmets.

INSULIN PUMPS

The Goddard Space Flight Center created a system to monitor astronauts' physical health while in space. This same technology led to a similar system now used to monitor blood sugar levels and release insulin to people with diabetes.

FLAME- AND HEAT-RESISTANT FIREFIGHTER SUITS

Some of the same technology developed for space suits and astronaut life support systems is now being used to create safer firefighter suits.

HAND-HELD VACUUM CLEANERS

NASA asked engineers at Black & Decker to work with them to invent battery-powered space tools for the Apollo moon landings. This led to the creation of the cordless, mini vacuum we now know as the Dustbuster.

LASIK CORRECTIVE EYE SURGERY

The same technology used to monitor astronauts' eyes during long visits to space is now being used to monitor a patient's eyes during surgery.

WATER FILTERING SYSTEMS

The same system that NASA developed in the 1970s to ensure astronauts had access to safe drinking water is the standard for water filtration systems today!

WIRELESS HEADSETS

NASA developed a lightweight, hands-free communication system to make it possible for astronauts aboard the Mercury and Apollo missions to communicate with mission control on Earth. Because of space research, we can now enjoy music and phone conversations without getting tangled up in cords!

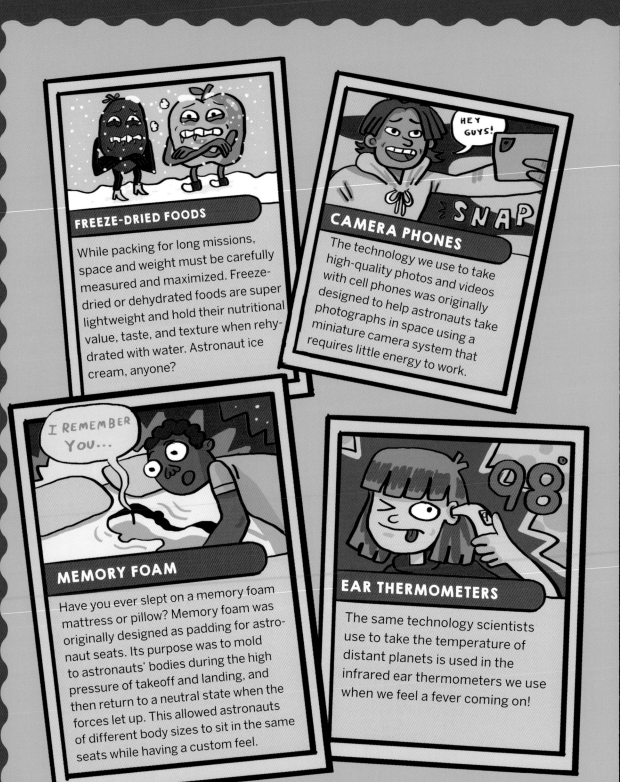

FREEZE-DRIED FOODS

While packing for long missions, space and weight must be carefully measured and maximized. Freeze-dried or dehydrated foods are super lightweight and hold their nutritional value, taste, and texture when rehydrated with water. Astronaut ice cream, anyone?

CAMERA PHONES

The technology we use to take high-quality photos and videos with cell phones was originally designed to help astronauts take photographs in space using a miniature camera system that requires little energy to work.

MEMORY FOAM

Have you ever slept on a memory foam mattress or pillow? Memory foam was originally designed as padding for astronaut seats. Its purpose was to mold to astronauts' bodies during the high pressure of takeoff and landing, and then return to a neutral state when the forces let up. This allowed astronauts of different body sizes to sit in the same seats while having a custom feel.

EAR THERMOMETERS

The same technology scientists use to take the temperature of distant planets is used in the infrared ear thermometers we use when we feel a fever coming on!

PORTABLE COMPUTERS

The first portable computer, nick-named SPOC (Shuttle Portable On-Board Computer), was used on space missions in the 1980s to do things like launch satellites off space shuttles. Now we use them to do homework!

3D FOOD PRINTING

The invention of 3D food printers has made it possible for astronauts to cook food on long space missions. Now they're being used here on Earth for all sorts of food, including the factory production of chocolates! Mmm-mmm!

ATHLETIC SHOES

Modern running shoe design was inspired by the shock-absorbing rubber originally invented for astronaut helmets.

SPACE PRANKS

Look, Mom! No Suits!

On April 1, 2010, three astronauts aboard the International Space Station beamed a photo to Mission Control on Earth featuring themselves floating *outside* its largest window. In the photo, the astronauts wore nothing but T-shirts, pants, sunglasses, and smiles.

While this might be acceptable attire on Earth, in space, with its extreme temperatures and lack of oxygen, the chances of surviving outside without proper space suits would be next to nothing! So why was everyone at Mission Control and the ISS laughing?

APRIL FOOLS! This digitally altered photo schemed up by NASA's Timothy Creamer, Japan's Soichi Noguchi, and Russian cosmonaut Oleg Kotov was the ultimate April Fools' space prank.

ultimate Hide-and-Seek

In 2017, NASA astronaut Peggy Whitson concocted an out-of-this-world prank to sneak up on her Russian crewmates. Since the ISS wasn't designed with hiding spots in mind, she convinced fellow astronauts Shane Kimbrough and Thomas Pesquet to pack her into a cargo bag and throw her into the Russian's module. When the other astronauts least expected it, she burst out

of the bag like a jack-in-the-box! Now that's how you make a surprise entrance!

Space Ape

In 2016, astronaut twins Mark and Scott Kelly devised a plan for some serious space shenanigans. Mark had a gorilla suit sent on a resupply flight to his brother, Scott, aboard the ISS. When Scott opened the package, he quickly put on the gorilla suit and hid himself in a soft-storage container. Just as fellow astronaut Tim Peake was strapping down the container, Scott the space gorilla popped out and chased the British astronaut around the cabin! The whole hilarious prank was caught on NASA video and beamed right back down to Earth.

DO YOU HAVE WHAT IT TAKES

TO BE A NASA ASTRONAUT?

Applicant Information

FULL NAME:

LAST _____ FIRST _____ MIDDLE _____

ADDRESS: _____

PHONE NUMBER: _____

ARE YOU A U.S. CITIZEN? ☐ YEP!   ☐ NOPE!

a. EDUCATION

DO YOU HAVE A MASTER'S DEGREE IN ANY OF THE FOLLOWING FIELDS?

☐ Biological Science   ☐ Engineering

☐ Computer Science   ☐ Math

☐ Physical Science   ☐ NOPE!

IF YOU ANSWERED **NOPE!** TO THE PREVIOUS QUESTION, DO YOU HAVE A MEDICAL DEGREE? ☐ YEP! ☐ NOPE!

HAVE YOU COMPLETED A TEST PILOT PROGRAM? ☐ YEP! ☐ NOPE!

HAVE YOU SPENT AT LEAST TWO YEARS WORKING ON A PHD IN SCIENCE, TECHNOLOGY, ENGINEERING, OR MATH? ☐ YEP! ☐ NOPE!

DO YOU HAVE AT LEAST 1,000 HOURS OF FLIGHT TIME AS A PILOT-IN-COMMAND ON A JET AIRCRAFT? ☐ YEP! ☐ NOPE!

IF YOU ANSWERED **NOPE!** DO YOU HAVE TWO YEARS OF EXPERIENCE DOING ANYTHING LIKE THAT? ANYTHING AT ALL? ☐ YEP! ☐ NOPE!

Does writing this book count?

NOPE!

b. PHYSICAL

ARE YOU BETWEEN 62 AND 75 INCHES TALL? ☐ YEP! ☐ NOPE!

ARE YOU PHYSICALLY FIT ENOUGH TO PASS
THE NASA ASTRONAUT PHYSICAL TEST? ☐ YEP! ☐ NOPE!

c. SKILLS

DO YOU CONSIDER YOURSELF A GOOD LEADER? ☐ YEP! ☐ NOPE!

DO YOU WORK WELL WITH OTHERS? ☐ YEP! ☐ NOPE!

DO YOU HAVE GOOD COMMUNICATION SKILLS? ☐ YEP! ☐ NOPE!

DO YOU EVEN WANT TO BE AN ASTRONAUT? ☐ YEP! ☐ NOPE!

ARE YOU STILL A KID? ☐ YEP! ☐ NOPE!

If you answered *YEP!* to the last question, we are sorry to say that you do not have what it takes to be an astronaut . . . YET! The good news is that you still have plenty of time! While you're waiting, here are some early steps you can take toward an out-of-this-world career in the future!

★ **Participate in science and engineering fairs:** Show off your experiments and discoveries and learn from others!

★ **Join or start a STEM club:** Get a head start on the hands-on education you'll need to become an astronaut and make it fun by doing it with friends who share your goals!

★ **Stay active or try a new sport:** Astronauts aboard the International Space Station exercise for *two hours* a day just to keep their bones strong for living life in microgravity!

The word **astronaut** comes from the Greek words meaning "star" and "sailor." Anyone who has trained to participate in spaceflight can be considered an astronaut.

WELCOME TO ASTRONAUT TRAINING SCHOOL

*Actual blast off may not occur for several years. Most of your time as an astronaut will be spent working on Earth.

NASA only accepts applications for astronaut school about every four years. In March 2020, NASA received more than 12,000 applications and only picked 10 candidates.

More than 550 people have been to space!

I like those odds!

DID YOU KNOW?

Did you know you can find how many people are in space right now? Visit **www.howmanypeopleareinspacerightnow.com** to find out!

A Day in the Life of an Astronaut on the International Space Station →

Ever since the Gemini mission in 1965, astronauts in space have been awakened every morning by songs played from Mission Control on Earth. Some past favorites have been "Come Fly with Me" by Frank Sinatra, "Rocket Man" by Elton John, "Space Oddity" by David Bowie, and several college fight songs.

Because the ISS orbits Earth 16 times during a 24-hour period, astronauts can enjoy as many as **16 sunrises and sunsets every single DAY!**

Gooooooood Morning!

It's 6:00 a.m. here on the International Space Station. An astronaut's workday begins at 6:00 a.m. and ends at 9:30 p.m. Greenwich Mean Time, which means that back at NASA's mission control centers in Houston, Texas, and Huntsville, Alabama, it's the middle of the night. Time to unstrap myself from the sleeping bag I've been in for the last eight hours!

Reporting for Doodie!

Upon waking, I spend a little time strapped to the toilet so I can do my "business." What's with all these straps and footholds and seatbelts, you ask? Well, *you* try sitting on a toilet in microgravity! Two words: FLYING FECES!

Lucky for us, our toilets operate with super suction power! Think of a toilet mixed with a vacuum cleaner that sucks air—and, uh . . . waste—into our sanitation tank. Also, we each have our own personal pee funnel attached to a hose that's attached to the toilet. Now, do you mind giving me some privacy?

Sometimes astronaut poop is brought back to Earth for scientists to study, but most of the time it's burned.

In 2018, NASA spent **$23 million** on a new and improved, two-part toilet for the ISS. It has a funnel and hose for peeing and a tiny, suction-powered toilet bowl for pooping!

Time to Shower!

And by "shower" I mean taking a sponge bath by squeezing a little pouch of soap into my hands, mixing it with a teeny-tiny bit of water, and washing up. For my hair, I use a rinseless shampoo. There's no running water on the ISS, and the water we do have is constantly being recycled so not a drop is wasted. That includes the moisture from our breath and even our pee! It's all purified through a filter so it can be used over and over again. I try not to think about it too much.

Breakfast Time!

Proper nutrition is important when you're living in microgravity for months at a time. A nutritionist on Earth helps plan our meals to make sure we're getting the vitamins and minerals we need. All our food is packaged in airtight containers. This packaging is flexible, easy to use, and helps keep our food from flying away! Some food can be eaten straight from the package, but others, like scrambled eggs, come dried up, with all of the water sucked out! In order to eat it, we have to add water and cook it. Wanna hear something nuts?

Our salt and pepper comes in *liquid* form! That's because shaking regular salt and pepper in space—without gravity—would be a disaster. It would fly everywhere, getting into the controls, up our noses, and into our eyes. Think of us the next time you dump salt all over your popcorn.

SPACE FOOD FACTS

★ The first food eaten in space was beef and liver paste squeezed from a tube. Astronaut food has come a long way since 1961!

★ There is no refrigerator on the ISS—yet. Several labs on Earth have designed microgravity refrigerators that are ready to be tested in space!

★ In 2019, astronauts on the ISS baked the first batch of space cookies. These five chocolate-chip cookies took over two hours to bake in zero gravity, but the astronauts didn't even get to eat them. The cookies were part of an experiment and had to be "tested for safety."

★ The ISS has an espresso machine! It was a gift from Italy in 2015 and is now known as the ISS-PRESSO machine.

Time to Hit the Gym!

Did you know that being an astronaut aboard the ISS means exercising for up to two and a half hours every single day? It's important to keep our bones and muscles strong, especially when living in zero gravity. We have some of the same exercise equipment found on Earth, only with special harnesses to keep us from floating away. And since a 200-pound (91 kg) weight up here might weigh nothing compared to how heavy it would feel on Earth, the ISS gym has special machines designed to give us the same resistance we'd find with gravity. Now please excuse me while I strap myself onto this treadmill for a brisk run.

Did you know that you can see the International Space Station from your own home? It's the third brightest object in the sky! Visit www.spotthestation.nasa.gov to find out when to look up and find it whizzing by!

Let's Get to Work!

Since the ISS is an orbiting space laboratory, we astronauts use our time here to study space! We experiment with microgravity, robotics, microorganisms, even our own bodies! It's also our job to take care of the place. We're responsible for daily chores, including cleaning, repairing, and updating. I guess you can say these chores make us feel right at home.

TO-DO LIST*:

* Develop a robot to help with dangerous tasks
* Watch flatworms grow two heads
* Grow space lettuce!
* Build a robotic mold-detecting nose
* Watch flames become great balls of fire FIRE!
* copy gecko feet to sticky robot feet

*These are all experiments that have been conducted on the ISS since 2000.

Lunchtime!

My favorite lunch has always been a peanut butter and banana sandwich. So you can imagine my horror when I was told that there is NO BREAD ALLOWED on the ISS! Apparently bread and its crumbs could cause major problems in microgravity. That's why I use tortillas instead! Tortillas are nutritious, plus they don't create crumbs, take up much room, get moldy, *or* need refrigeration. In fact, they can stay fresh on a shelf for up to 18 months! They're kind of the perfect space food. (They're not too bad on Earth either!)

Bathroom Break!

If you think it's in bad taste to fart in front of other people on Earth, imagine what it's like when you let one rip on the ISS! At least on Earth, air helps move the gas around until the smell goes away. But up here, in close quarters with very little air-flow, the stench just hangs around! That's why we try to do all of our farting in the bathroom, where there's a little more ventilation.

Dinnertime!

Did you know all our food packages come with Velcro attached? It helps keep our food on the table while we eat. Otherwise it would—you guessed it—float away! And take a look at this menu! There are 200 carefully chosen foods and drinks to choose from, including some of our favorites from back home on Earth.

Actual foods served on the ISS!

MENU

APPETIZERS
CORN CHOWDER
SHRIMP COCKTAIL
BACON SQUARES

MAIN DISHES
PORK AND SCALLOPED POTATOES
SPAGHETTI WITH MEAT SAUCE
MACARONI AND CHEESE

DESSERTS
BUTTERSCOTCH PUDDING
PINEAPPLE FRUIT CAKE
BROWNIES

DRINKS
GRAPE PUNCH
ORANGE GRAPEFRUIT DRINK
ORANGE DRINK

I tried to order takeout, but the price was astronomical!

GROAN

Free Time!

Even astronauts take breaks to have fun! And while we can't necessarily play outside, here are some things we can do:

- STARE OUT THE WINDOW AND SPY ON EARTH.
- PRANK OUR CREWMATES.
- GO FOR A CABIN FLOAT.
- PLAY WITH OUR FOOD.
- CALL OUR FAMILIES BACK ON EARTH.

Bedtime!

Whew! What a day! Each crew member has a cabin where we're scheduled to sleep for eight hours a night. Because of microgravity, we can't sleep in beds like we do on Earth. Here, we strap ourselves into special sleeping bags that hold us in place so we don't bump into things while we're asleep. And since there's no up or down in microgravity, we can sleep in any direction we want!

And there you have it! A day in the life on the International Space Station. Thanks for visiting! Good night and sleep tight!

Anatomy of a Space Suit

Gloves: Two layers! One layer for comfort and an outer layer with rubberized fingertips to help you grip objects found during space exploration!

Helmet: Equipped with a patch of Velcro to scratch your nose if you have an itch!

Extravehicular Visor Assembly (EVA): Like sunglasses, but for your whole face! The EVA is tough enough to protect you from any mini-meteoroids that may come your way. It also comes equipped with four headlamps and a camera to record everything you encounter on your space walk.

In-Suit Drink Bag: Astronauts need water too! This bag full of potable water is connected to a mouthpiece by a long tube, allowing for on-demand hydration.

Communications Carrier Assembly: A fabric cap worn under the helmet. It's installed with microphones and earphones so you can communicate with your crewmates and mission control, hands-free!

Hard Upper Torso: This hard shell made of fiberglass helps to support your arms, torso, helmet, life-support backpack, tools, and control module.

Display and Control Module: This control panel has everything you need to access the features on your primary life support system. A little mirror on your sleeve will help you to see the buttons without your big helmet getting in the way.

Maximum Absorption Garment: It's a space diaper! Going on a long, seven-hour space walk and don't want to worry about finding the nearest restroom? Just poop and pee your pants!

Liquid Cooling and Ventilation Garment: Long undies equipped with plastic water tubes connected to a backpack. These tubes will help cool you down during those sweaty space walks.

EMU Electrical Harness: One-stop shop for connecting *all* your devices.

Primary Life Support System: A big backpack filled with everything you need to survive your space walk, including oxygen, electrical power, cooling fans, drinking water, and a warning system.

Lower Torso Assembly: Everything from the waist down—lower pants, knee and ankle joints, and boots. It's fitted to the upper half with a metal ring.

Secondary Oxygen Pack: Because you can never have too much backup for the one thing you need to survive!

Arms: Complete with a cheat sheet printed on the sleeve to remind you of your space walk to-do checklist!

WHAT'S BEEN SENT BEFORE US

Whoa! Ready to feel a little beef'd?! Here are a bunch of objects that were sent to space before us!*

LEGO MINIFIGURES
The mythological god Jupiter, his wife, Juno, and Italian astronomer Galileo all got to go to Jupiter! *And* they rode there on NASA's Juno space probe! LUCKY!

A GOLDEN RECORD
Aliens, if you're out there, this is for you! This timeless album contains hits such as "Natural Sounds from Earth like Thunder, Wind, Birds, Whales," as well as classics like "Music from Different Cultures and Periods of History" and—of course—a bonus track with greetings from humans in 55 languages!

A CORNED BEEF SANDWICH
Bread isn't allowed in space, but that didn't stop astronaut John Young from smuggling one aboard the Gemini 2 space mission!

AMELIA EARHART'S WATCH

The first woman to fly solo across the Atlantic is also the first woman to have her watch sent to space—82 years to the day after her historic transatlantic flight, in 2014. It should also be noted that by the time it arrived, the time was all wrong!

> Sorry, watch, you're on GMT time now, baby!

LUKE SKYWALKER'S LIGHTSABER!

Okay, to be fair, this one *should* be in space. This original lightsaber from *Return of the Jedi* was blasted up to the International Space Station in 2007 to mark the 30th anniversary of the *Star Wars* movies. Can you believe that none of the astronauts on board used it to engage in any epic Jedi battles?! In fact, they never even took it out of the box. BOO!

> I think it's supposed to be symbolic.

A SALAMI PIZZA?!

Special delivery! When a Russian cosmonaut was living aboard the International Space Station, he developed a craving for pizza. But what do you do when you're about 250 miles (402 km) *above* the nearest Pizza Hut? You have it delivered via space rocket! While the pizza only cost a few bucks, the delivery charge was more than $1,000,000! Hope he left a good tip!

A TESLA

HONK HONK

That's right! To mark the first launch of SpaceX's Falcon Heavy rocket in 2018, the red electric sports car was released into outer space, with David Bowie's songs "Space Oddity" and "Life on Mars?" playing on repeat on the car's stereo. It's been traveling at speeds of more than 6,000 miles (9,656 km) per hour on a solar orbit toward Mars ever since!

*Don't worry, you may not be a salami pizza, but you still have plenty of time.

SPACE ODDITIES

SPACE TOOLS

Wow! Look at all this bonkerballs space stuff, Guy Raz!

I know, Mindy, where should we start?

POD 4 SALE

BOGO

50% OFF

ZERO GRAVITY 3D PRINTER

In 2014, NASA brought a 3D printer to the ISS. Then astronauts were able to 3D print a usable ratchet wrench, the first tool ever manufactured in space. The goal is to eventually use the printer to print replacement parts for the space station—a much cheaper option than shipping them from Earth.

3D PRINTER, BARELY USED, WORKS IN ZERO GRAVITY

3D-TRON

Don't get me started on those interstellar delivery fees!

ROBONAUT

Robonaut, as the name suggests, is half robot, half astronaut. Robonaut lives on the ISS, and with its humanlike arms and hands, it is able to operate most of the same tools that real astronauts use. It's remote-controlled using a specialized 3D visor and gloves by either engineers on Earth or astronauts on the ISS.

In 2014, Robonaut was given legs! It can now perform even more demanding space tasks, such as moonwalking.

Say hello to a human's best friend!

ROBONAUT. REMOTE-CONTROLLED. COMES WITH OR WITHOUT LEGS

ADVANCED RESISTIVE EXERCISE DEVICE

Astronauts who spend a lot of time in space risk losing up to 15 percent of their muscle mass if they don't keep up a strict exercise routine. To do this, they use a specialized machine that allows them to weight lift in a weightless environment or during suborbital flight. There's also a treadmill that straps them in for running.

ADVANCED RESISTIVE EXERCISE DEVICE
PUT ON WEIGHT...EVEN WHEN YOU'RE WEIGHT-LESS! MAX RESISTANCE: 600 POUNDS (272 KG)!

Oooooh, a treadmill.

Ummmm, actually it's an Advanced Resistive Exercise Device.

MOBILE SERVICING SYSTEM (CANADARM)

That big robotic arm hanging off the side of the ISS? It's known as the Canadarm because the Canadian government paid for this bonkerballs space gadget! These long, robotic arms are found all over the ISS. The Canadarm is 57.7 feet (17.6 m) long when fully extended and contains seven joints, making it extremely flexible. And it's capable of carrying up to 200,000 pounds (90,718 kg) of stuff!

MADE IN CANADA
SRP $896 MILLION
ONBOARD AUTOMATIC COLLISION AVOIDANCE SYSTEM

OOOOOOO Canada . . .

WATER RECLAMATION SYSTEM

Launched in 2008, the Water Reclamation System collects the wastewater on the ISS—including the astronauts' urine, condensation from walls and windows, and used shower water—and purifies it using a series of filtration systems. The end result is 100 percent safe drinking water.

Perfect for water cooler conversations!

Drinking your own pee! GROSS!

Don't knock it 'til you've tried it!

PEE-RIFIER

FILTERS YOUR PEE! GETS RID OF THE BAD STUFF! GOOD FOR BOTH DRINKING AND BATHING!

PISTOL-GRIP TOOL

This cordless power drill was specially designed for use on the Hubble Space Telescope, but has since been used to make repairs on the ISS. It features a handle designed to be used with the thick gloves of a space suit, a rechargeable battery, a display screen, and the ability to withstand a 500° temperature change!

$$$

SPATULA

Used exactly once on July 12, 2006, by astronaut Piers Sellers, who was using this spatula to test heat tile putty.

$FREE.99

While this tool could have had a long, useful life in space, it slipped from Sellers's hands and sadly burned upon reentry into Earth's atmosphere.

GLOSSARY

Accretion disk A ring of dust, gas, and other space particles surrounding a very large, still-growing celestial body, such as a planet, star, or black hole.

Asteroid Space rocks that orbit the sun! They're smaller than planets but come in all shapes and sizes: as little as 33 feet to more than 300 miles in diameter.

Astronaut A person who is trained to travel into space. In Greek, "astro" means star and "naut" means sailor, so astronauts are basically star sailors!

Astronomer A scientist who studies space.

Atmosphere A layer of gas surrounding a planet.

Binary stars Two stars orbiting each other. (Or sometimes a pair of stars orbiting the same large object.)

Black hole A place in space where gravity is so strong that nothing can escape—not even light!

Comet An icy object that orbits the sun. The sun's heat makes passing comets release a trail of gas that looks like a tail.

Constellation A group of stars identified by a specific pattern or shape, often associated with Roman and Greek mythology.

Cosmonaut A Russian astronaut. In Greek, "cosmo" means universe and "naut" means sailor. (In the 1960s, the Soviet Union and the United States both wanted to be first to reach the moon. The two countries picked different names for their space travelers so everyone in the world could tell them apart.)

Crater A bowl-shaped pit left behind by a meteorite, volcanic eruption, or explosion.

Dark energy or **dark matter** Mysterious, invisible stuff in space that has gravity. It is estimated to make up 95 percent of the universe, but scientists are still trying to figure out what it's made of and how it works!

Dark sky zone An area protected from artificial light so the stars are easier to see and study. Also called dark sky preserves.

Dwarf planet A celestial body that is large enough to be squeezed into a spherical shape (bigger than an asteroid), but not large enough to clear other objects from its orbit (smaller than a regular planet).

Earth Our home planet! The third planet from the sun in our solar system.

Enceladus One of Saturn's 82 moons! It's as small as the state of Arizona, but scientists think it has the right conditions for life.

Europa One of Jupiter's 79 moons! It's a little smaller than Earth's moon, but it may have a salty ocean beneath its icy surface and other conditions suitable for hosting life.

Event horizon The boundary of a black hole, or the point of no return! Once the event horizon is crossed, nothing—not even light—can escape.

Exoplanet A planet orbiting a star that is not the sun.

Extraterrestrial Something out of this world! An extraterrestrial being is a life-form not from Earth. Sometimes these are also called aliens.

Galaxy A huge collection of gas, dust, and stars held together by gravity.

Gas giant A planet without a hard outer surface made of gases, like hydrogen and helium, pulled toward a dense, solid core. Jupiter and Saturn are gas giants!

Goldilocks Zone An area near a star where it is not too hot or too cold for liquid water. Also called a "habitable zone," conditions for extraterrestrial life in these areas are juuuust right. (Just like the story of *The Three Bears*!)

Gravity The force by which a planet or other body draws objects toward its center. For example, the sun's gravity keeps the planets in orbit and Earth's gravity keeps us on the ground.

Ice giant A large planet with a big, icy rock core and slushy, gassy surface. Unlike gas giants, these are made of heavier elements, like oxygen, carbon, nitrogen, and sulfur. Neptune and Uranus are ice giants.

International Space Station (ISS) A large spacecraft with a laboratory inside that orbits Earth about 250 miles above the surface. Astronauts from different countries live there for a few weeks at a time while performing experiments and taking space walks.

James Webb Space Telescope The largest, most powerful space telescope ever built! It launched December 25, 2021. Scientists use it to study the early universe and some of the first galaxies ever formed.

Jupiter The fifth planet from the sun and the largest planet in our solar system. It's a gas giant that's mostly made of helium and hydrogen.

Kepler Space Telescope A retired space telescope launched in 2009.

Light pollution When artificial light causes bad effects on the environment. Too much artificial light can also make it hard to see or study stars at night.

Light-year The distance light travels in one year. It's the same as 5,878,499,810,000 miles! It's easier to describe distant objects in light-years instead of millions, billions, or trillions of miles away.

Mars The fourth planet from the sun. Mars is a rocky planet with lots of iron oxide in its soil, which makes it look rusty. That's why it's called the Red Planet.

Mercury The closest planet to the sun, and also the smallest. This rocky planet has a heavy iron core.

Meteor A bright streak of light created by a chunk of rock or metal from space burning up in a planet's atmosphere.

Meteorite If a meteor reaches Earth's surface, it is called a meteorite.

Meteoroid Any chunk of rock or metal from space that reaches Earth's atmosphere.

Microgravity Very weak gravity! It's why astronauts appear weightless in spacecraft or on a space walk.

Milky Way Our home galaxy and a spiral galaxy. The Milky Way is approximately 100,000 light-years across and contains at least 100 billion stars!

Moon Earth's only natural satellite!

Moons Solid celestial bodies that orbit planets, dwarf planets, and asteroids in our solar system. (Exo-moons orbit objects outside of our solar system!)

NASA National Aeronautics and Space Administration. It's the space research agency of the United States government.

Nebula A giant cloud of dust and gas in space where stars are born.

Neptune The farthest planet from the sun. Neptune is an ice giant with the fastest winds in the solar system.

Neutron star Some of the densest objects in the universe. They form after the matter from a large star collapses in on itself before exploding in a supernova. Neutron stars are small—usually just 12 miles across, the size of a small city.

Nuclear fusion How stars are born. Nuclear fusion happens when hydrogen is converted into helium. It expels a huge amount of energy, resulting in a lot of heat and a lot of light!

Orbit The path of an object around a particular point in space, defined by gravity.

Planet A large body in outer space that circles around a star.

Planet X Scientists have found mathematical evidence of a possible ninth planet in the solar system. In theory, it could be about 20 times farther from the sun than Neptune. It would take this planet 20,000 years to complete a lap around the Sun!

Pluto A dwarf planet orbiting the sun near Neptune. It was considered the ninth planet until 2006, when it was reclassified.

Protostar A baby star or, technically, a cloud of gas and dust in space that eventually develops into a star.

Quasar An object near the center of a galaxy that produces a lot of light. Quasars are usually found near black holes and are some of the brightest objects in the universe!

Red giant A star near the end of its life cycle that has run out of hydrogen to convert to helium, which is necessary to maintain nuclear fusion. At this stage, it can expand more than 100 times its original size.

Relativistic jet A black hole burp! Black holes sometimes spit radiation and particles into space. They can be several light-years long.

Robonaut A NASA robot built to resemble a person. It uses tools to help out on the ISS.

Rocket A device that produces enough force to launch spacecraft.

Satellite A small object orbiting a large object.

Saturn The sixth planet from the sun and a gas giant known for its rings.

SETI Institute Scientists working together to Search for Extra-Terrestrial Intelligence.

Singularity The incredibly dense center of a black hole.

Solar mass A unit used to measure the mass of stars. It is equal to the size of our sun.

Solar system The sun and everything that orbits it! It's our galactic neighborhood.

Space Anything outside Earth's atmosphere.

Spacecraft A vehicle or device designed to be used outside Earth's atmosphere.

Space shuttle A reusable spacecraft used to transport people and cargo between Earth and space.

Spaghettification The effect on an object that gets stretched or ripped apart by the gravitational forces of a black hole.

Star A huge, glowing ball of gas made mostly of hydrogen and powered by nuclear fusion. Our sun is a star!

Sun The glowing ball of gas at the center of our solar system.

Supernova The violent, explosive death of a star. A supernova occurs when a star's core collapses under the weight of its own gravity.

Telescope An instrument that uses curved glass, light, and mirrors to allow people to see distant objects.

Universe Everything that exists, including objects and energy, throughout time and space.

Uranus The seventh planet from the sun and an ice giant that spins on its side!

Venus The second planet from the sun. This rocky planet is also the solar system's hottest.

White dwarf The final evolutionary state of a star that isn't heavy enough to turn into a neutron star. Gravity has compacted the star into the size of Earth, with the mass of the sun.

BIBLIOGRAPHY AND RECOMMENDED READING

Aguilar, David A. *Space Encyclopedia, 2nd Edition: A Tour of Our Solar System and Beyond.* Washington, D.C.: National Geographic Kids, 2020.

Arlon, Penelope. *Space!: The Universe as You've Never Seen It Before.* New York: DK Publishing, 2021.

Dinwiddie, Robert; Couper, Heather; et al. *Planets: The Definitive Visual Guide to Our Solar System.* New York: DK Publishing, 2014.

Lonely Planet. *The Universe: A Travel Guide.* Wilson, WY: Lonely Planet, 2019.

Regas, Dean. *1,000 Facts About Space.* Washington, D.C.: National Geographic Kids, 2022.

RECOMMENDED LISTENING

Have your grown-up scan these QR codes to listen to some of our favorite out-of-this-world episodes of *Wow in the World*.

Lucy the Space Ar-chaeologist

Betelgeuse! Betel-geuse! Betelgeuse! An Outer Space SUPERNOVA

Two-Headed Space Worms

Spaced Out Pen Pal: Part 1

Spaced Out Pen Pal: Part 2

Astronauts, Clean Up Your Outer Space!

**An Elevator
to the Stars!**

**MY ASTEROID
IS BLOWING UP!**

**Martian
Beach Party**

**Tour of
Titan**

**Is There Life
on Venus?**

**Mini-
Moon!**

**An Inter-galactic
Interloper!**

**Hey Mars!
Put a Ring
on It!**

**The Very Hungry
Black Hole**

SOURCE NOTES

PART I: THE UNIVERSE

Once upon a time: European Space Agency. "The Big Bang." Last updated June 20, 2014. https://www.esa.int/kids/en/learn/Our_Universe/Story_of_the_Universe/The_Big_Bang.

The pressure inside: European Space Agency. "The Big Bang." Last updated June 20, 2014. https://www.esa.int/kids/en/learn/Our_Universe/Story_of_the_Universe/The_Big_Bang.

At first, it was: Erickson, Kristen. "What Is the Big Bang?" NASA Space Place. Last updated March 17, 2021. https://spaceplace.nasa.gov/big-bang/en/.

The cold turned: European Space Agency. "The Big Bang." Last updated June 20, 2014. https://www.esa.int/kids/en/learn/Our_Universe/Story_of_the_Universe/The_Big_Bang.

At first, those atoms: Dorling Kindersley. "The Big Bang." DK Findout! Accessed October 14, 2021. https://www.dkfindout.com/us/space/stars-and-galaxies/big-bang/.

But soon gravity: Dorling Kindersley. "The Big Bang." DK Findout! Accessed October 14, 2021. https://www.dkfindout.com/us/space/stars-and-galaxies/big-bang/.

Then, our baby universe: Dorling Kindersley. "The Big Bang." DK Findout! Accessed October 14, 2021. https://www.dkfindout.com/us/space/stars-and-galaxies/big-bang/.

The sun: Barnett, Amanda. "Solar System Exploration." NASA Solar System Exploration. Last updated April 19, 2022. https://solarsystem.nasa.gov/solar-system/sun/overview/#otp_overview.

The solar system: Barnett, Amanda. "Solar System Exploration." NASA Solar System Exploration. Last updated April 19, 2022. https://solarsystem.nasa.gov/solar-system/sun/overview/#otp_overview.

To help keep track: Guharay, Deboleena M. "A Brief History of the Periodic Table." *ASBMB Today.* February 7, 2021. https://www.asbmb.org/asbmb-today/science/020721/a-brief-history-of-the-periodic-table.

The periodic table: Britannica Kids. "Periodic Table." *Encyclopaedia Britannica.* Accessed October 21, 2021. https://kids.britannica.com/kids/article/periodic-table/600334.

The lightest element is: Resnick, Brian. "4 New Elements Will Be Added to the Periodic Table. Here's What It Means." *Vox.* January 4, 2016. https://www.vox.com/science-and-health/2016/1/4/10709760/new-elements-periodic-table.

Some of these elements: Science Learning Hub. "How Elements Are Formed." University of Waikato. October 22, 2009. https://www.sciencelearn.org.nz/resources/1727-how-elements-are-formed.

Supernovas happen: Erickson, Kristen. "What Is a Supernova?" NASA Space Place. Last updated July 23, 2021. https://spaceplace.nasa.gov/supernova/en/.

Once a star: Mattson, Barbara. "Stars." NASA Imagine the Universe! Last updated September 23, 2021. https://imagine.gsfc.nasa.gov/science/objects/stars1.html.

This creates new: Johnson-Groh, Mara. "Souped-Up Supernovas May Produce Much of the Universe's Heavy Elements." *Science News.* July 7, 2021. https://www.sciencenews.org/article/star-explosion-hypernova-supernova-universe-heavy-elements-origin.

Elements cannot be created: Encyclopedia Britannica. "The Conservation of Matter." Accessed October 21, 2021. https://www.britannica.com/science/principle-of-microscopic-reversibility.

Every time an element: Mattson, Barbara. "The Dispersion of Elements." NASA Imagine the Universe! Last updated March 8, 2017. https://imagine.gsfc.nasa.gov/educators/lessons/xray_spectra/background-elements.html.

It's most likely: Lotzof, Kerry. "Are We Really Made of Stardust?" Natural History Museum. Accessed October 21, 2021. https://www.nhm.ac.uk/discover/are-we-really-made-of-stardust.html.

A galaxy is: Erickson, Kristen. "What Is a Galaxy?" NASA Space Place. Last updated June 4, 2020. https://spaceplace.nasa.gov/galaxy/en/.

Galaxies can come: Kiddle. "Galaxy Facts for Kids." Kids Encyclopedia Facts. Last modified April 29, 2022. https://kids.kiddle.co/Galaxy.

There are three main: Mattson, Barbara. "Galaxies." NASA Imagine the Universe! September 23, 2021. https://imagine.gsfc.nasa.gov/science/objects/galaxies1.html#:~:text=Galaxies%20are%20classified%20by%20shape,elliptical%2C%20spiral%2C%20and%20irregular.

These galaxies are flat: Hubblesite. "Galaxies." NASA Space Telescope Science Institute. Accessed October 22, 2021. https://hubblesite.org/science/galaxies#:~:text=Spiral%20galaxies%20appear%20as%20flat,runs%20through%20the%20central%20bulge.

have arms that flare: Erickson, Kristen. "Types of Galaxies." NASA Space Place. Last updated June 4, 2020. https://spaceplace.nasa.gov/galactic-explorer/en/.

Two thirds of observed: Greshko, Michael. "Galaxies, Explained." *National Geographic*. April 17, 2019. https://www.nationalgeographic.com/science/article/galaxies?loggedin=true.

Our home galaxy: American Museum of Natural History. "The Milky Way Galaxy." Accessed October 22, 2021. https://www.amnh.org/explore/ology/astronomy/the-milky-way-galaxy2#:~:text=The%20Milky%20Way%20is%20a,the%20center%20of%20the%20galaxy.

It's approximately: Mattson, Barbara. "The Cosmic Distance Scale." NASA Imagine the Universe! October 22, 2020. https://imagine.gsfc.nasa.gov/features/cosmic/milkyway_info.html#:~:text=The%20Milky%20Way%20is%20about,Arm%20of%20the%20Milky%20Way.

These make up almost: Erickson, Kristen. "Types of Galaxies." NASA Space Place. Last updated June 24, 2020. https://spaceplace.nasa.gov/galaxy/en/.

Some are circular: Howell, Elizabeth. "What Are Elliptical Galaxies?" Space.com. January 9, 2019. https://www.space.com/22395-elliptical-galaxies.html.

Irregular Galaxy: Kiddle. "Irregular Galaxy Facts for Kids." Kids Encyclopedia Facts. Last modified April 9, 2022. https://kids.kiddle.co/Irregular_galaxy.

That makes scientists: Hubblesit. "Galaxies." NASA Space Telescope Science Institute. Accessed October 22, 2021. https://hubblesite.org/science/galaxies.

It only interacts: Erickson, Kristen. "Dark Matter." NASA Space Place. Last updated June 27, 2019. https://spaceplace.nasa.gov/dark-matter/en/.

Around 500 million: Dorling Kindersley. "The Big Bang." DK Findout! Accessed October 24, 2021. https://www.dkfindout.com/us/space/stars-and-galaxies/big-bang/.

When these gasses combust: Choi, Charles Q. "Simple Recipe for Star Formation Revealed." Space.com. April 10, 2014. https://www.space.com/25434-star-formation-recipe-revealed.html.

before you know it: Hubblesite. "Galaxies." NASA Space Telescope Science Institute. Accessed October 22, 2021. https://hubblesite.org/science/galaxies.

Scientists believe that: Hille, Karl. "Hubble Reveals Observable Universe Contains 10 Times More Galaxies Than Previously Thought." NASA. October 13, 2016. https://www.nasa.gov/feature/goddard/2016/hubble-reveals-observable-universe-contains-10-times-more-galaxies-than-previously-thought.

Some are light enough: NASA. "How Gravity Warps Light." NASA Tumblr. Accessed October 30, 2021. https://nasa.tumblr.com/post/187009797389/how-gravity-warps-light.

The sun is not only: Barnett, Amanda. "Our Sun." NASA Science Solar System Exploration. Accessed October 30, 2021. https://solarsystem.nasa.gov/solar-system/sun/in-depth/#:~:text=The%20Sun%20is%20the%20largest,debris%20in%20orbit%20around%20it.

at 109 times wider: Greshko, Michael. "The Sun, Explained." *National Geographic*. September 15, 2018. https://www.nationalgeographic.com/science/article/the-sun?loggedin=true.

it's also the heaviest: The Nine Planets. "The Sun Fact." Last updated January 4, 2021. https://nineplanets.org/the-sun/.

The sun weighs: Sharp, Tim, and Ailsa Harvey. "How Big Is the Sun?" Space.com. January 21, 2022. https://www.space.com/17001-how-big-is-the-sun-size-of-the-sun.html.

This is often referred: Woo, Marcus. "What Is Solar Mass?" Space.com. December 6, 2018. https://www.space.com/42649-solar-mass.html.

It lies about 163,000 light-years: Tillman, Nora Taylor. "What Is the Most Massive Star?" Space.com. July 28, 2018. https://www.space.com/41313-most-massive-star.html.

for the past few million years: European Southern Observatory. "Stars Just Got Bigger." July 21, 2010. https://www.eso.org/public/usa/news/eso1030/.

Neutron stars are: Greicius, Tony, and Naomi Hartono. "Different Types of Neutron Stars." NASA Jet Propulsion Laboratory. June 24, 2020. https://www.jpl.nasa.gov/images/pia23863-different-types-of-neutron-stars-illustration.

Although they're typically: Naeye, Robert. "Neutron Stars." NASA FERMI. August 23, 2007. https://www.nasa.gov/mission_pages/GLAST/science/neutron_stars.html.

Neutron stars are created: Mattson, Barbara. "Neutron Stars." NASA Imagine the Universe! Last updated September 23, 2021. https://imagine.gsfc.nasa.gov/science/objects/neutron_stars1.html.

One of the larger: Finley, Dave. "Astronomers Discover Most Massive Neutron Star Yet Known." National Radio Astronomy Observatory. October 27, 2010. https://www.nrao.edu/pr/2010/bigns/.

Although it's only: Nerlich, Steve. "Astronomy Without a Telescope—Cubic Neutrons." Universe Today. August 20, 2011. https://www.universetoday.com/88311/astronomy-without-a-telescope-cubic-neutrons/.

weight of 2 solar masses: Özel, Feryal, Dimitrios Psaltis, Scott Ransom, Paul Demorest, and Mark Alford. "The Massive Pulsar PSR J1614-2230: Linking Quantum Chromodynamics, Gamma-Ray Bursts, and Gravitational Wave Astronomy." *Astrophysical Journal Letters* 724, no. 2 (December 1, 2010): L199–L202. https://doi.org/10.1088/2041-8205/724/2/L199.

Black holes are so heavy: European Space Agency. "Black Holes." Last modified June 14, 2016. https://www.esa.int/kids/en/learn/Our_Universe/Story_of_the_Universe/Black_Holes.

There are four: Wei-Haas, Maya. "Black Holes, Explained." *National Geographic*. Accessed October 30, 2021, https://www.nationalgeographic.com/science/article/black-holes.

Although all black holes: Wild, Flint. "What Is a Black Hole?" NASA Knows! Last updated August 21, 2018. https://www.nasa.gov/audience/forstudents/k-4/stories/nasa-knows/what-is-a-black-hole-k4.html.

there's a supermassive black hole: Boen, Brooke. "Supermassive Black Hole Sagittarius A*." NASA. Last updated August 7, 2017. https://www.nasa.gov/mission_pages/chandra/multimedia/black-hole-SagittariusA.html.

TON 618 was: Byrd, Deborah. "Hefty Black Hole Holds New Record for High Mass." EarthSky, December 8, 2019. https://earthsky.org/space/astronomers-discover-heaviest-black-hole-abell85-nearby-universe/.

242 billion miles (390 billion km) across: Silvertant, Martin. "The Largest Object in the Universe." Medium. January 17, 2020. https://medium.com/@msilvertant/the-largest-object-in-the-universe-810dc829668f.

864,000 miles (1.4 million km) wide: Dunbar, Brian. "The Sun." NASA. Last updated August 3, 2017. https://www.nasa.gov/sun.

I'm the smallest planet: Erickson, Kristen. "All About Mercury." NASA Space Place. Last updated September 1, 2021. https://spaceplace.nasa.gov/all-about-mercury/en/.

But I spin slowly: Erickson, Kristen. "How Long Is One Day on Other Planets?" NASA Space Place. Last updated February 9, 2021. https://spaceplace.nasa.gov/days/en/.

I basically have no atmosphere: Barnett, Amanda. "Mercury." NASA Solar System Exploration. Last updated October 19, 2021. https://solarsystem.nasa.gov/planets/mercury/in-depth/#:~:text=Temperatures%20on%20Mercury%20are%20extreme,(minus%20180%20degrees%20Celsius.

I spin backwards: Barnett, Amanda. "Venus." NASA Solar System Exploration. Accessed May 19, 2022. https://solarsystem.nasa.gov/planets/venus/overview/.

Hey, Earth neighbor: Britannica Kids. "Venus." *Encyclopaedia Britannica*. Accessed October 20, 2021. https://kids.britannica.com/kids/article/Venus/353895#.

Venus here, hottest planet: Erickson, Kristen. "All About Venus." NASA Space Place. Last updated September 1, 2021. https://spaceplace.nasa.gov/all-about-venus/en/.

hanging out after dark: Mangum, Jeff. "Ask an Astronomer." National Radio Astronomy Observatory. October 6, 2020. https://public.nrao.edu/ask/why-is-venus-visible-in-the-night-sky-when-its-orbit-is-closer-to-the-sun/#:~:text=Answer%3A,only%20during%20these%20times%20also.

I am your closest neighbor: Flanders, Tony. "Don't Miss the Brightest Objects in the Night Sky." *Sky & Telescope*. February 22, 2012. https://skyandtelescope.org/astronomy-news/observing-news/see-the-6-or-7-brightest-night-objects/.

volcano capital of the solar system: "Volcano World: Venus." Oregon State University. Accessed October 30, 2021. https://volcano.oregonstate.edu/venus.

covered in poisonous clouds: Barnett, Amanda. "Venus." NASA Solar System Exploration. Accessed May 19, 2022. https://solarsystem.nasa.gov/planets/venus/overview/.

I've been around for 4.5 billion: National Geographic Resource Library. "Age of the Earth." Accessed October 30, 2021. https://education.nationalgeographic.org/resource/resource-library-age-earth.

the Goldilocks Zone: Brennan, Pat. "What Is the Habitable Zone or 'Goldilocks Zone'?" NASA Exoplanet Exploration. Accessed October 30, 2021. https://exoplanets.nasa.gov/faq/15/what-is-the-habitable-zone-or-goldilocks-zone/#:~:text=The%20habitable%20zone%20is%20the,the%20surface%20of%20surrounding%20planets.&text=The%20distance%20Earth%20orbits%20the,zone%2C%20or%20the%20Goldilocks%20zone.

Water: NASA. "Ocean Worlds." Accessed October 30, 2021. https://www.nasa.gov/specials/ocean-worlds/.

A quirky little tilt: National Geographic Resource Library. "Axis." Accessed October 30, 2021. https://education.nationalgeographic.org/resource/axis.

It might have rained: Wall, Mike. "Mars' Raindrops May Once Have Been Bigger Than Earth's." Space.com. May 18, 2017. https://www.space.com/36893-mars-rain-climate-atmosphere-evolution.html.

Mars here: Barnett, Amanda. "Mars." NASA Solar System Exploration. Accessed October 30, 2021. https://solarsystem.nasa.gov/planets/mars/overview/.

which is basically just rust: Good, Andrew, and Alana Johnson. "The Moon Is Rusting, and Researchers Want to Know Why." NASA, Last updated September 4, 2020. https://www.nasa.gov/feature/jpl/the-moon-is-rusting-and-researchers-want-to-know-why.

I have really bad dust storms: Mersmann, Kathryn. "The Fact and Fiction of Martian Dust Storms." NASA. Last updated August 7, 2017. https://www.nasa.gov/feature/goddard/the-fact-and-fiction-of-martian-dust-storms.

three times the height of Mount Everest: Wonderopolis. "Where Is the Highest Mountain?" National Center for Families Learning. Accessed November 2, 2021. https://wonderopolis.org/wonder/where-is-the-highest-mountain.

almost 16 miles (26 km): NASA's Mars Exploration Program. "Olympus Mons." Accessed November 2, 2021. https://mars.nasa.gov/gallery/atlas/olympus-mons.html.

Two cute little moons: Barnett, Amanda. "Mars Moons." NASA Solar System Exploration. Accessed November 3, 2021. https://solarsystem.nasa.gov/moons/mars-moons/in-depth/.

Their names are Phobos and Deimos: Tillman, Nola Taylor. "Mars' Moons: Facts About Phobos & Deimos." Space.com, December 7, 2017. https://www.space.com/20413-phobos-deimos-mars-moons.html.

the smallest in the solar system: Barnett, Amanda. "Mars Moons." NASA Solar System Exploration. Accessed November 3, 2021. https://solarsystem.nasa.gov/moons/mars-moons/in-depth/.

the biggest planet in the solar system: Erickson, Kristen. "All About Jupiter." NASA Space Place. Last updated September 1, 2021. https://spaceplace.nasa.gov/all-about-jupiter/en/.

1,000 times bigger than Earth: Britannica Kids. "Jupiter." *Encyclopaedia Britannica*. Accessed October 20, 2021. https://kids.britannica.com/kids/article/Jupiter/353328.

I'm gassy: Erickson, Kristen. "All About Jupiter." NASA Space Place. Last updated September 1, 2021. https://spaceplace.nasa.gov/all-about-jupiter/en/.

I'm bright: The Nine Planets. "Jupiter Facts for Kids." Accessed November 2, 2021. https://nineplanets.org/kids/jupiter/.

I have the biggest moon: Barnett, Amanda. "Ganymede." NASA Solar System Exploration. Accessed November 30, 2021. https://solarsystem.nasa.gov/moons/jupiter-moons/ganymede/overview/.

It's a storm so big: Go, Christopher. "Jupiter's Great Red Spot Swallows Earth." NASA Jet Propulsion Laboratory. July 11, 2017. https://www.jpl.nasa.gov/images/pia21774-jupiters-great-red-spot-swallows-earth.

It used to be: Paoletta, Rae. "The Shape of Jupiter's Great Red Spot Is Changing. Here's Why." The Planetary Society. October 7, 2021. https://www.planetary.org/articles/why-jupiter-great-red-spot-changing-shape.

Saturday was named: Coolman, Robert. "Origins of the Days of the Week." LiveScience. May 7, 2014. https://www.livescience.com/45432-days-of-the-week.html.

the jewel of the solar system: NASA Jet Propulsion Laboratory. "Jewel of the Solar System: Part 1—What Do I See When I Picture Saturn?" Accessed November 2, 2021. https://www.jpl.nasa.gov/edu/teach/activity/jewel-of-the-solar-system.

Others may know me: Erickson, Kristen. "All About Saturn." NASA Space Place. Last updated September 1, 2021. https://spaceplace.nasa.gov/all-about-saturn/en/.

Let's just say I am nine times: Britannica Kids. "Saturn." *Encyclopaedia Britannica*. Accessed November 2, 2021. https://kids.britannica.com/kids/article/Saturn/353745.

In fact, it's possible: Erickson, Kristen. "All About Saturn." NASA Space Place. Last updated September 1, 2021. https://spaceplace.nasa.gov/all-about-saturn/en/.

It's pronounced YOOR-un-us: Lakdawalla, Emily. "On the Pronunciation of 'Uranus.' " The Planetary Society. January 12, 2009. https://www.planetary.org/articles/1806.

My name is Uranus: Stern, Albert. "A Deep Dive into Uranus Jokes." Electric Lit. November 17, 2017. electricliterature.com/a-deep-dive-into-uranus-jokes/.

Like rotten eggs: Michaud, Peter, and Jasmin Silva. "What Do Uranus's Cloud Tops Have in Common with Rotten Eggs?" Gemini Observatory. Last updated April 25, 2018. https://www.gemini.edu/pr/what-do-uranus-s-cloud-tops-have-common-rotten-eggs.

mixed with toots: Mandelbaum, Ryan F. "Confirmed: Uranus Smells Like Farts." Gizmodo. April 23, 2018. https://gizmodo.com/stinky-molecules-confirm-uranus-smells-like-farts-1825467106.

I'm actually an ice giant: Erickson, Kristen. "All About Uranus." NASA Space Place. Last updated September 1, 2021. https://spaceplace.nasa.gov/all-about-uranus/en/.

I just happen to have all these: Irwin, Patrick G. J., Daniel Toledo, Ryan Garland, Nicholas A. Teanby, Leigh N. Fletcher, Glenn A. Orton, and Bruno Bézard. "Detection of Hydrogen Sulfide above the Clouds in Uranus's Atmosphere." *Nature Astronomy* no. 2 (April 23, 2018): 420–427. https://www.nature.com/articles/s41550-018-0432-1.

I've also got wind speeds: Barnett, Amanda. "Uranus." NASA Solar System Exploration. Accessed November 30, 2021. https://solarsystem.nasa.gov/planets/uranus/in-depth/.

I can proudly declare myself: The Nine Planets. "Uranus Facts for Kids." Accessed November 2, 2021. https://nineplanets.org/kids/uranus/.

My swirling clouds of methane gas: Kraus, D., Vorberger, J., Pak, A. et al. "Formation of Diamonds in Laser-Compressed Hydrocarbons at Planetary Interior Conditions." *Nature Astronomy* no. 1 (August 21, 2017): 606–617. https://www.nature.com/articles/s41550-017-0219-9.

I'm super far from the sun: Barnett, Amanda. "Neptune." NASA Solar System Exploration, Accessed November 4, 2021. https://solarsystem.nasa.gov/planets/neptune/in-depth/.

I've got winds: National Weather Service. "The Planet Neptune." Accessed November 4, 2021. https://www.weather.gov/fsd/neptune#:~:text=The%20highest%20winds%20observed%20in,of%20sound%20here%20on%20Earth.

Every few years, a storm: Kiddle. "Great Dark Spots Facts for Kids." Kids Encyclopedia Facts. Last modified July 16, 2021. https://kids.kiddle.co/Great_Dark_Spot.

all the broken pieces from the collision: Lotzof, Kerry. "How Did the Moon Form?" Natural History Museum. Accessed November 5, 2021. https://www.nhm.ac.uk/discover/how-did-the-moon-form.html.

4.5 billion years: Barboni, Melanie, Patrick Boehnke, Brenhin Keller et al. "Early Formation of the Moon 4.51 Billion Years Ago." *Science Advances* 3, no. 1 (2017). https://www.science.org/doi/10.1126/sciadv.1602365.

I've already been walked on: Barnett, Amanda. "Who Has Walked on the Moon?" NASA Solar System Exploration. April 28, 2021. https://solarsystem.nasa.gov/news/890/who-has-walked-on-the-moon/.

In fact, I'm the only place: Barnett, Amanda. "Earth's Moon: Our Natural Satellite." NASA Solar System Exploration. Accessed November 4, 2021. https://solarsystem.nasa.gov/moons/earths-moon/in-depth/.

I'm about 1/4: Dyches, Preston. "Five Things to Know about the Moon." NASA Solar System Exploration. July 28, 2021. https://solarsystem.nasa.gov/news/1946/five-things-to-know-about-the-moon/.

I'm also pretty low: van Loon, Jacco. "Curious Kids: How High Could I Jump on the Moon?" The Conversation. July 25, 2019. https://theconversation.com/curious-kids-how-high-could-i-jump-on-the-moon-120865.

And my gravitational pull: National Geographic Resource Library. "Tide." Accessed November 4, 2021. https://education.nationalgeographic.org/resource/tide.

I'm slowly moving away: Koren, Marina. "The Moon Is Leaving Us." *The Atlantic*. September 30, 2021. https://www.theatlantic.com/science/archive/2021/09/moon-moving-away-earth/620254//.

Don't worry, it's less: BBC News. "Why the Moon is Getting Further Away from Earth." February 1, 2011, https://www.bbc.com/news/science-environment-12311119.

Earth and I are totally: Barnett, Amanda. "Earth's Moon." NASA Solar System Exploration. Accessed November 4, 2021. https://solarsystem.nasa.gov/moons/earths-moon/overview/.

really long moonquakes: LaFrance, Adrienne. "Moonquakes and Marsquakes." *The Atlantic*. September 21, 2015. https://www.theatlantic.com/technology/archive/2015/09/moonquakes-and-marsquakes/406516/.

You should see its craters: Erickson, Kristen. "Why Does the Moon Have Craters?" NASA Space Place. Last updated April 23, 2020. https://spaceplace.nasa.gov/craters/en/.

Astronomers think it would take around 20,000: Barnett, Amanda. "Hypothetical Planet X." NASA Solar System Exploration. Accessed November 4, 2021. https://solarsystem.nasa.gov/planets/hypothetical-planet-x/in-depth/.

We have thousands of: Brennan, Pat. "How Many Exoplanets Are There?" NASA Exoplanet Exploration. Accessed November 5, 2021. https://exoplanets.nasa.gov/faq/6/how-many-exoplanets-are-there/.

51 Pegasi b: Brennan, Pat. "51 Pegasi b," NASA Exoplanet Exploration. Accessed November 5, 2021. https://exoplanets.nasa.gov/exoplanet-catalog/7001/51-pegasi-b/.

About the same mass: Brennan, Pat. "Proxima Centauri b." NASA Exoplanet Exploration. Accessed November 5, 2021. https://exoplanets.nasa.gov/exoplanet-catalog/7167/proxima-centauri-b/.

One side of the planet: Kekesi, Alex. "Earth Versus Proxima Centauri b Rotation Rates." NASA Scientific Visualization Studio. January 23, 2020. https://svs.gsfc.nasa.gov/4778.

And a point where it's: Siegel, Ethan. "Ten Ways 'Proxima b' Is Different From Earth." *Forbes*, September 6, 2016. https://www.forbes.com/sites/startswithabang/2016/09/06/ten-ways-proxima-b-is-different-from-earth/?sh=3c048f0f59c7.

About a third: Brennan, Pat. "Kepler-16b." NASA Exoplanet Exploration. Accessed November 5, 2021. https://exoplanets.nasa.gov/exoplanet-catalog/1814/kepler-16b/.

Here on Kepler-16b: Drake, Nadia. "On Kepler-16b, Shadows Come in Pairs." *Science News*. September 15, 2011. https://www.sciencenews.org/article/kepler-16b-shadows-come-pairs.

two sunrises each and every day: Ornes, Stephen. "Double Sunsets on a Distant World." *Science News for Students*. October 5, 2011. https://www.sciencenewsforstudents.org/article/double-sunsets-distant-world.

But unlike our solar system: Brennan, Pat. "NASA Telescope Reveals Largest Batch of Earth-Size, Habitable-Zone Planets around Single Star." NASA Exoplanet Exploration. February 21, 2017. https://exoplanets.nasa.gov/news/1419/nasa-telescope-reveals-largest-batch-of-earth-size-habitable-zone-planets-around-single-star/.

This means that if you were: Landau, Elizabeth. "10 Things: All About TRAPPIST-1." NASA Solar System Exploration. February 20, 2018. https://solarsystem.nasa.gov/news/335/10-things-all-about-trappist-1/.

Most of these planets: NOAA. "Exoplanet: TRAPPIST-1e." Science on a Sphere. Accessed November 5, 2021. https://sos.noaa.gov/catalog/datasets/exoplanet-trappist-1e/.

This is the area around: Brennan, Pat. "What is the Habitable Zone or 'Goldilocks zone'?" NASA Exoplanet Exploration. Accessed November 5, 2021. https://exoplanets.nasa.gov/faq/15/what-is-the-habitable-zone-or-goldilocks-zone/.

The Kepler Space Telescope: Dooling, Dave. "Kepler." *Enclopaedia Britannica*. Accessed November 5, 2021. https://www.britannica.com/topic/Kepler-satellite.

Since then it's discovered: Brennan, Pat. "Kepler's Legacy: Discoveries and More." NASA Exoplanet Exploration. Accessed November 4, 2021. https://exoplanets.nasa.gov/keplerscience/.

More than half of all: Wall, Mike. "1,000 Alien Planets! NASA's Kepler Space Telescope Hits Big Milestone." Space.com. January 6, 2015. https://www.space.com/28105-nasa-kepler-spacecraft-1000-exoplanets.html.

Launched in 2022: Fisher, Alise. "Following Webb's Arrival at L2, Telescope Commissioning Set to Begin." *NASA James Webb Space Telescope* (blog). January 31, 2022. https://blogs.nasa.gov/webb/2022/01/31/following-webbs-arrival-at-l2-telescope-commissioning-set-to-begin/.

although we've discovered: Brennan, Pat. "How Many Exoplanets Are There?" NASA Exoplanet Exploration. Accessed November 4, 2021. https://exoplanets.nasa.gov/faq/6/how-many-exoplanets-are-there/.

But many astronomers think: The Bryant Park Project. "Astronomers on Verge of Finding Earth's Twin." NPR. June 25, 2008. https://www.npr.org/templates/story/story.php?storyId=91868324.

When you consider space travel's: The Editors of Encyclopaedia Britannica. "Neil Armstrong." *Encyclopaedia Britannica*. Accessed November 5, 2021. https://www.britannica.com/biography/Neil-Armstrong.

Fruit Fly: First Living: Royal Museums Greenwich. "What Was the First Animal Sent into Space?" Accessed November 4, 2021. https://www.rmg.co.uk/stories/topics/what-was-first-animal-space.

These brave insects: Harrington, Monica. "Fruit Flies in Space." *Lab Animal* 43, no. 3 (January 2014): 3. https://www.nature.com/articles/laban.451.

The edge of space: NASA Share the Science. "The Edge of Space." July 24, 2021. https://science.nasa.gov/edge-space.

This research came in handy: Mai, Thuy. "April 196—First Human Entered Space." NASA. Last updated September 7, 2018. https://www.nasa.gov/directorates/heo/scan/images/history/April1961.html.

Great apes such as chimpanzees: Groves, Colin Peter. "Ape." *Encyclopaedia Britannica*. Accessed November 5, 2021. https://www.britannica.com/animal/ape.

Ham the Chimpanzee: Save the Chimps. "Ham, the First Chimpanzee in Space." Accessed November 5, 2021. https://savethechimps.org/ham-space-chimp/.

three whole months before Yuri Gagarin: History.com Editors. "Soviet Cosmonaut Yuri Gagarin Becomes the First Man in Space." History.com. February 9, 2010. https://www.history.com/this-day-in-history/first-man-in-space.

Alan Shepard, the first American: Mars, Kelli. "60 Years Ago: Alan Shepard Becomes the First American in Space." NASA History. Last updated May 5, 2021. https://www.nasa.gov/image-feature/60-years-ago-alan-shepard-becomes-the-first-american-in-space.

On July 16, 1969: History.com Editors. "1969 Moon Landing." History.com. Last updated May 14, 2021. https://www.history.com/topics/space-exploration/moon-landing-1969.

A half year before that: NASA. "Apollo 8: Christmas at the Moon." December 23, 2019. https://www.nasa.gov/topics/history/features/apollo_8.html.

Like the moon!: Wild, Flint. "What Is an Orbit?" NASA. Last updated August 7, 2017. https://www.nasa.gov/audience/forstudents/5-8/features/nasa-knows/what-is-orbit-58.html.

Hope the Cockroach: Whitesides, Loretta Hidalgo. "Cockroach Births First Babies Conceived in Space." Wired. October 24, 2007. https://www.wired.com/2007/10/cockroach-birth/.

PART II: STARS

The most stars: Garber, Megan. "How Many Stars Are There in the Sky?" *The Atlantic*. November 19, 2013. https://www.theatlantic.com/technology/archive/2013/11/how-many-stars-are-there-in-the-sky/281641/.

Over time, gravity: NASA Goddard Space Flight Center. "Stars." Imagine the Universe! Last updated February 2014. https://imagine.gsfc.nasa.gov/science/objects/stars1.html.

Once that protostar: Kiddle. "Protostars Facts for Kids." Kiddle Encyclopedia. Last modified July 16, 2021. https://kids.kiddle.co/Protostar#:~:text=Protostar%20is%20an%20early%20stage,temperature%20than%20an%20ordinary%20star.

This expels a huge: NASA Share the Science. "Stars." Last updated June 30, 2022. https://science.nasa.gov/astrophysics/focus-areas/how-do-stars-form-and-evolve.

This phase of life: Swinburne University of Technology. "Protostar." Cosmos. Accessed November 5, 2021. https://astronomy.swin.edu.au/cosmos/p/Protostar#:~:text=During%20this%20time%2C%20and%20up,of%20the%20star%20being%20formed.

Once nuclear fusion: The StarChild Team. "Stars." NASA StarChild. Accessed November 5, 2021. https://starchild.gsfc.nasa.gov/docs/StarChild/universe_level2/stars.html#:~:text=Once%20its%20mass%20is%20stabilized,and%20it%20starts%20to%20contract.

Stars will spend: Australia Telescope National Facility. "Main Sequence Stars." CSIRO. Accessed November 5, 2021. https://www.atnf.csiro.au/outreach/education/senior/astrophysics/stellarevolution_mainsequence.html#:~:text=Main%2DSequence%20Lifespan,evolving%20into%20a%20red%20giant.

Once the star runs out of fuel: NASA Goddard Space Flight Center. "The Life Cycles of Stars." Imagine the Universe! Last updated May 7, 2015. https://imagine.gsfc.nasa.gov/educators/lifecycles/LC_main3.html.

These are much smaller: The Editors of Encyclopaedia Britannica, "White Dwarf Star," *Encyclopaedia Britannica*. Accessed November 4, 2021. https://www.britannica.com/science/white-dwarf-star.

The immense heat: Swinburne University of Technology. "White Dwarf." Cosmos. Accessed November 4, 2021. https://astronomy.swin.edu.au/cosmos/W/white+dwarf.

If the star is particularly: NASA Goddard Space Flight Center. "The Life Cycles of Stars." Imagine the Universe! Last updated May 7, 2015. https://imagine.gsfc.nasa.gov/educators/lifecycles/LC_main3.html.

Our sun is: CalTech, "Which Star Is Closest to Us?" Cool Cosmos. Accessed November 6, 2021. https://coolcosmos.ipac.caltech.edu/ask/208-Which-star-is-closest-to-us-#:~:text=The%20closest%20star%20to%20us,miles%20(about%2039%2C900%2C000%2C000%2C000%20kilometers.

The next closest: Sharp, Tim. "Alpha Centauri: Closest Star to Earth." Space.com. November 5, 2021. https://www.space.com/18090-alpha-centauri-nearest-star-system.html.

There may be as many: Masetti, Maggie. "How Many Stars in the Milky Way?" NASA Goddard Space Flight Center. July 22, 2015. https://asd.gsfc.nasa.gov/blueshift/index.php/2015/07/22/how-many-stars-in-the-milky-way/.

And they call me the Secondary Star: Space.com Staff. "Binary Star Systems: Classification and Evolution." Space.com. January 17, 2018. https://www.space.com/22509-binary-stars.html.

Binary Stars are two stars: Australia Telescope National Facility. "Binary Stars." CSIRO. Accessed November 5, 2021. https://www.atnf.csiro.au/outreach/education/senior/astrophysics/binary_intro.html.

SAO 206462 is located: Space.com Staff. "Spiral Dust Clouds May Reveal Alien Planets." Space.com. December 1, 2012. https://www.space.com/19001-spiral-dust-clouds-alien-planets.html.

The arms are made: Phillips, Tony. "A Star with Spiral Arms." NASA Share the Science. Last updated June 30, 2022. https://science.nasa.gov/science-news/science-at-nasa/2011/31oct_spiralarms.

Over the next several million years: NASA Jet Propulsion Laboratory. "Cultivating a Planetary Garden: How Long Does it Take?" September 12, 2005. https://www.jpl.nasa.gov/news/cultivating-a-planetary-garden-how-long-does-it-take.

Stars can come: Malik, Tariq. "Hubble Telescope Spots Red, White and Blue Stars in Sparkly Cluster." Space.com. July 4, 2021. https://www.space.com/hubble-telescope-red-white-blue-stars-photo.

The bigger the star: Temming, Maria. "How Do Stars Die and How Long Do Stars Live?" *Sky & Telescope*. July 15, 2014. https://skyandtelescope.org/astronomy-resources/how-long-do-stars-live-stars-die/#:~:text=A%20star's%20life%20expectancy%20depends,few%20million%20years%20of%20fusion.

Lucy is a star in: Futurism, "Lucy's in the Sky with Diamonds: Meet the Most Expensive Star Ever Found." June 12, 2014. https://futurism.com/lucy-in-the-sky-with-diamonds.

it weighs as much as the sun: Coverly, JD. "Look! A Diamond the Size of the Moon!" Wonder How To. September 16, 2010. https://science.wonderhowto.com/news/look-diamond-size-moon-0120376/.

a temperature of 10,832°F (6,000°C): BBC News. "Diamond Star Thrills Astronomers." February 16, 2004. http://news.bbc.co.uk/2/hi/3492919.stm.

In comparison, our sun: Barnett, Amanda. "Sun." NASA Solar System Exploration. Last updated April 19. 2022. https://solarsystem.nasa.gov/solar-system/sun/overview/#:~:text=The%20temperature%20in%20the%20Sun's ,enough%20to%20sustain%20nuclear%20fusion.

Scientists have predicted: National Geographic. "White Dwarf." Accessed November 4, 2021. https://www .nationalgeographic.com/science/article/white-dwarfs?loggedout=true.

The shimmering you see: Temming, Maria. "Why Do Stars Twinkle?" *Sky & Telescope*. July 15, 2014. https:// skyandtelescope.org/astronomy-resources/why-do-stars-twinkle/.

Well known to astronomers: NASA Jet Propulsion Laboratory. "Summer Triangle Corner: Vega," Night Sky Network. Last updated June 1, 2020. https://nightsky.jpl.nasa.gov/news-display.cfm?News_ID=912.

That's because of its high: Sessions, Larry, and Deborah Byrd. "Summer Triangle Star: Vega Is Bright and Blue-White." EarthSky. July 2, 2021. https://earthsky.org/brightest-stars/vega-brilliant-blue-white-is-third-brightest-star/.

Vega may be twice: Plait, Phil. "A Planet for Vega?" SyFy. March 15, 2021. https://www.syfy.com/syfy-wire/a-planet-for -vega.

Our sun takes 27: The Nine Planets. "Vega (Lyrae) Facts." Last updated January 4, 2021, https://nineplanets.org/ vega-%CE%B1-lyrae/.

If you're stargazing: Sessions, Larry. "Top 10 Cool Things about Stars." EarthSky. May 24, 2016. https://earthsky.org/ space/ten-things-you-may-not-know-about-stars/.

named after the oldest man: Noyes, Penny. "Who Was Methuselah in the Bible?" Christianity.com. April 24, 2019. https://www.christianity.com/wiki/people/who-was-methuselah-in-the-bible.html.

That means this star: Crookes, David. "Methuselah: The Oldest Star in the Universe." Space.com. March 7, 2022. https://www.space.com/how-can-a-star-be-older-than-the-universe.html.

If you tried to hitch: Fazekas, Andrew. "Inside the Quest for a Real 'Star Trek' Warp Drive." *National Geographic*. October 29, 2016. https://www.nationalgeographic.com/science/article/star-trek-warp-drive-interstellar-travel-space -astronomy-science.

We've used the stars: National Geographic Resource Library. "Navigation." Accessed November 6, 2021. https:// education.nationalgeographic.org/resource/navigation.

Well, you have to use: Taggart, Emma. "10 Legendary Constellations and the Stories Behind Them (According to Greek Mythology)." My Modern Met. May 15, 2021. https://mymodernmet.com/famous-constellations/.

Well, the big star says: NASA. "Earth Observatory." July 24, 2000. https://earthobservatory.nasa.gov/features/ StarsCloudsCrops.

Venus is easy to find: Wei-Haas, Maya. "Venus, Explained." *National Geographic*. Accessed November 4, 2021. https:// www.nationalgeographic.com/science/article/venus-1?loggedin=true.

Venus should be visible: Carter, Jamie. "Venus Is at Its Brightest Ever This Week—Here's How to See It." *Travel + Leisure*. April 23, 2020. https://www.travelandleisure.com/trip-ideas/space-astronomy/viewing-bright-venus-april-2020#.

Sirius is the brightest star: Howell, Elizabeth, and Ailsa Harvey. "Sirius: The Brightest Star in Earth's Night Sky." Space .com. January 27, 2022. https://www.space.com/21702-sirius-brightest-star.html.

It shimmers with other: Byrd, Deborah. "See Sirius, the Brightest Star in the Night Sky." EarthSky. February 7, 2021. https://earthsky.org/brightest-stars/sirius-the-brightest-star/.

This reddish-looking star: The Editors of Encyclopaedia Britannica. "Betelgeuse." *Encyclopaedia Britannica*. Accessed November 6, 2021. https://www.britannica.com/place/Betelgeuse-star.

Betelgeuse can be seen: The Observatory Science Centre. "Andromeda Galaxy." Night Sky Objects. Accessed November 5, 2021. https://www.the-observatory.org/night-sky-objects.

The largest constellation: Gregersen, Erik. "Hydra." *Encyclopaedia Britannica*. Accessed November 5, 2021. https:// www.britannica.com/place/Hydra-constellation.

A constellation named: Britannica Kids. "Hercules." *Encyclopaedia Britannica*. Accessed November 5, 2021. https:// kids.britannica.com/students/article/Hercules/341205.

It is named after Orion: Zimmermann, Kim Ann, and Daisy Dobrijevic. "Orion Constellation: Facts, Location and Stars of the Hunter." Space.com. November 4, 2021. https://www.space.com/16659-constellation-orion.html.

Ursa Major: Britannica Kids. "Ursa Major." *Encyclopaedia Britannica*. Accessed November 5, 2021. https://kids .britannica.com/students/article/Ursa-Major/313956.

More commonly known as the Southern Cross: Rao, Joe. "Exploring the Famous Southern Cross Constellation." Space.com. May 19, 2015. https://www.space.com/29445-southern-cross-constellation-skywatching.html.

It can weigh anywhere: The Editors of Encyclopaedia Britannica. "Black Hole." *Encyclopaedia Britannica*. Accessed November 5, 2021. https://www.britannica.com/science/black-hole.

And all of this is squeezed: NASA Goddard Space Flight Center. "Black Holes." Imagine the Universe! Last updated September 23, 2021. https://imagine.gsfc.nasa.gov/science/objects/black_holes1.html.

That's why they're: McMaster, Adam, and Andrew Norton. "Astronomers May Have Spotted an 'Invisible' Black Hole for the First Time." LiveScience. February 14, 2022. https://www.livescience.com/invisible-black-hole-discovered.

As the stars get closer: Wei-Haas, Maya. "Black Holes, Explained." *National Geographic*. Accessed November 5, 2021. https://www.nationalgeographic.com/science/article/black-holes.

Quasars are some: Britannica Kids. "Quasars." *Encyclopaedia Britannica*. Accessed November 5, 2021. https://kids.britannica.com/students/article/quasar/276613.

Gravity increases the closer: Oxford Reference. "Spaghettification." Accessed November 5, 2021. https://www.oxfordreference.com/view/10.1093/acref/9780198609810.001.0001/acref-9780198609810-e-6655.

For example, if you: Orwig, Jessica. "10 Mind-Blowing Facts About Black Holes." *Business Insider*. October 19, 2014. https://www.businessinsider.com/what-black-holes-really-are-2014-10.

Stellar black holes: NASA Share the Science. "Black Holes." Last updated June 30, 2022. https://science.nasa.gov/astrophysics/focus-areas/black-holes.

They are often formed: NASA. "A New Kind of Black Hole." November 30, 2007. https://www.nasa.gov/vision/universe/starsgalaxies/Black_Hole.html.

Not too small: Wiegert, Theresa. "A New Goldilocks Black Hole." EarthSky. April 1, 2021. https://earthsky.org/space/intermediate-black-hole-gravitational-lens-gamma-ray-burst/.

They typically lurk: European Space Agency. "Black Holes." Last modified June 14, 2016. https://www.esa.int/kids/en/learn/Our_Universe/Story_of_the_Universe/Black_Holes.

Supernovas are a star's: Erickson, Kristen. "What Is a Supernova?" NASA Space Place. Last updated July 23, 2021. https://spaceplace.nasa.gov/supernova/en/.

If the star is large enough: BBC. "The Life Cycle of a Star." Bite Size. Accessed November 5, 2021. https://www.bbc.co.uk/bitesize/guides/zpxv97h/revision/1.

Time moves slower: Harvard Smithsonian Center for Astrophysics. "A Black Hole Is a One-Way Exit from Our Universe." Universe Forum. Accessed November 5, 2021. https://lweb.cfa.harvard.edu/seuforum/bh_whatare.htm.

This is because the sextant: Casual Navigation. "How Sextants Work: An Illustrated Guide." Accessed November 7, 2021. https://casualnavigation.com/how-sextants-work-an-illustrated-guide/.

First invented by world renowned: Library of Congress, "Galileo and the Telescope," Finding Our Place in the Cosmos: From Galileo to Sagan and Beyond. Accessed November 5, 2021. https://www.loc.gov/collections/finding-our-place-in-the-cosmos-with-carl-sagan/articles-and-essays/modeling-the-cosmos/galileo-and-the-telescope.

Did you know he: Rice University. "Pendulum Clock." The Galileo Project. Accessed November 6, 2021. http://galileo.rice.edu/sci/instruments/pendulum.html.

Our expertly crafted: Erickson, Kristen. "How Do Telescopes Work?" NASA Space Place, Last updated September 30, 2021. https://spaceplace.nasa.gov/telescopes/en/#:~:text=Most%20telescopes%2C%20and%20all%20large,light%20from%20the%20night%20sky.&text=The%20bigger%20the%20mirrors%20or,we%20look%20into%20the%20telescope.

This works as a sort: Ling, Samuel J., Jeff Sanny, and William Moebs. "Microscopes and Telescopes." In *University Physics*, Volume 3, Houston, Texas: OpenStax. 2016. https://opentextbc.ca/universityphysicsv3openstax/chapter/microscopes-and-telescopes/#:~:text=(b)%20Most%20simple%20refracting%20telescopes,inverted%20image%20that%20is%20magnified

The most important thing: Evans, Katrin Raynor. "Deep-Sky Astronomy: A Beginner's Guide." *BBC Sky at Night Magazine*. August 19, 2019. https://www.skyatnightmagazine.com/advice/skills/deep-sky-astronomy-beginners-guide/.

It's often created by buildings: Brown, Daniel. "How to See Stars and Tackle Light Pollution in Your Own Backyard." *The Conversation*. November 8, 2019. https://theconversation.com/how-to-see-stars-and-tackle-light-pollution-in-your-own-backyard-125005.

This means that they: Carter, Jamie. "10 U.S. Dark-Sky Parks You Need to Visit." *Sky & Telescope*, April 16, 2018. https://skyandtelescope.org/astronomy-blogs/astronomy-holidays-stargazing-tour/10-dark-sky-parks-in-the-u-s-you-need-to-visit/.

According to a study: Instituto de Astrofísica de Canarias (IAC). "The Natural Brightness of the Night Sky." May 6, 2021. https://www.eurekalert.org/news-releases/773368.

Scientists have predicted: Curious Kids. "How Many Stars Are There in Space?" The Conversation. September 20, 2021. https://theconversation.com/how-many-stars-are-there-in-space-165370.

PART III: SPACE ROCKS!

There are about 1 million: Barnett, Amanda. "Asteroids." NASA Solar System Exploration. Updated July 19, 2021. https://solarsystem.nasa.gov/asteroids-comets-and-meteors/asteroids/in-depth/.

Asteroids are typically: Erickson, Kristen. "What Is an Asteroid?" NASA Space Place. Last updated August 26, 2021. https://spaceplace.nasa.gov/asteroid/en/.

The asteroid that slammed: Britannica Kids. "Chicxulub Crater." *Encyclopaedia Britannica*. Accessed November 6, 2021. https://kids.britannica.com/students/assembly/view/107893.

That's about the size: The Empire State Building. "Empire State Building at a Glance." Accessed November 6, 2021. https://www.esbnyc.com/about/facts-figures.

Comets are like asteroids: Barnett, Amanda. "Comets." NASA Solar System Exploration. Accessed November 6, 2021. https://solarsystem.nasa.gov/asteroids-comets-and-meteors/comets/overview/?page=0&per_page=40&order=name+asc&search=&condition_1=102%3Aparent_id&condition_2=comet%3Abody_type%3Ailike.

In fact, the word comet: fresch.1."Word Study Activities for Home Schooling." *Fresch_Ideas* (blog), The Ohio State University. April 7, 2020. https://u.osu.edu/fresch.1/category/vocabulary/#:~:text=Ancient%20Greek%3A%20%E2%80%9Ckometes%E2%80%9D%20%E2%80%93,made%20its%20way%20to%20English.

A meteoroid is just: Erickson, Kristen. "Asteroid or Meteor: What's the Difference?" NASA Space Place. Last updated June 30, 2021. https://spaceplace.nasa.gov/asteroid-or-meteor/en/.

Meteoroids range in size: National Museum of Natural History. "Meteorites: Messengers from Outer Space." Smithsonian Institution. Accessed November 6, 2021. https://naturalhistory.si.edu/education/teaching-resources/earth-science/meteorites-messengers-outer-space.

Friction causes them: ESA Kids. "Meteors." European Space Agency. Last modified April 12, 2017. https://www.esa.int/kids/en/learn/Our_Universe/Comets_and_meteors/Meteors#:~:text=Small%20chunks%20of%20rock%20that,surface%20are%20known%20as%20meteorites.

Meteor showers happen: Erickson, Kristen. "What Is a Meteor Shower?" NASA Space Place. Last updated July 25, 2018. https://spaceplace.nasa.gov/meteor-shower/en/.

Something sudden, brilliant: Collins Dictionary. "Meteoric." Accessed November 6, 2021. https://www.collinsdictionary.com/us/dictionary/english-thesaurus/meteoric.

On June 30, 1908: Tedesco, Edward F. "Tunguska event." *Encyclopaedia Britannica*. Accessed November 6, 2021. https://www.britannica.com/place/Siberia.

That's half the size: Lemons, J. Stanley. "Rhode Island." *Encyclopaedia Britannica*. Accessed November 6, 2021. https://www.britannica.com/place/Rhode-Island-state.

Experts have estimated: Scotti, Monique. "NASA Plans Mission to a Metal-Rich Asteroid Worth Quadrillions." *Global News*. Updated January 16, 2017. https://globalnews.ca/news/3175097/nasa-plans-missi,on-to-a-metal-rich-asteroid-worth-quadrillions/.

The majority of the asteroids: Erickson, Kristen. "What Is an Asteroid?" NASA Space Place. Last updated July 25, 2018. https://spaceplace.nasa.gov/asteroid/en/.

One cluster is just: NASA. "Lucy: The First Mission to the Trojan Asteroids." Last updated September 27, 2021. https://www.nasa.gov/mission_pages/lucy/overview/index.

Most of these are: Barnett, Amanda. "Kuiper Belt." NASA Solar System Exploration. Updated November 16, 2021. https://solarsystem.nasa.gov/solar-system/kuiper-belt/overview/#.

Planets always orbit around a star: Merriam-Webster. "Planet." Accessed November 6, 2021. https://www.merriam-webster.com/dictionary/planet.

However, many smaller objects: NASA Share the Science. "Small Bodies of the Solar System." Last updated July 1, 2022. https://science.nasa.gov/solar-system/focus-areas/small-bodies-solar-system.

When this happens: Lotzof, Kerry. "How Did the Moon Form?" The Natural History Museum. Accessed November 6, 2021. https://www.nhm.ac.uk/discover/how-did-the-moon-form.html.

Here on Earth: Barnett, Amanda. "Saturn Moons." NASA Solar System Exploration. Accessed November 6, 2021. https://solarsystem.nasa.gov/moons/saturn-moons/overview/?page=0&per_page=40&order=name+asc&search=&placeholder=Enter+moon+name&condition_1=38%3Aparent_id&condition_2=moon%3Abody_type%3Ailike&condition_3=moon%3Abody_type.

Dwarf planets are: Brookshire, Bethany. "Scientists Say: Dwarf Planet." *Science News for Students*, March 20, 2017. https://www.sciencenewsforstudents.org/article/scientists-say-dwarf-planet.

Has cleared other objects: International Astronomical Union. "Pluto and the Developing Landscape of Our Solar System." Accessed November 6, 2021. https://www.iau.org/public/themes/pluto/.

You'll be joining: Barnett, Amanda. "Our Solar System." NASA Solar System Exploration. Updated December 8, 2017. https://solarsystem.nasa.gov/resources/490/our-solar-system/.

PART IV: ALIEN LIFE (?)

But some scientists: Soter, Steven, and Neil deGrasse Tyson (eds.). "Case Study: Fossil Microbes on Mars?" American Museum of Natural History. Accessed November 6, 2021. https://www.amnh.org/learn-teach/curriculum-collections/cosmic-horizons-book/fossil-microbes-mars.

The search for extraterrestrial: NASA's Mars Exploration Program. "Signs of Life on Mars? NASA's Perseverance Rover Begins the Hunt." July 20, 2021. https://mars.nasa.gov/news/8994/signs-of-life-on-mars-nasas-perseverance-rover-begins-the-hunt/.

Perseverance has been: NASA Mars 2020 Mission Perseverance Rover. "Mars 2020 Mission Overview." Accessed November 7, 2021. https://mars.nasa.gov/mars2020/mission/overview/.

It's an ancient lake bed: NASA Mars 2020 Mission Perseverance Rover. "Perseverance Rover's Landing Site: Jezero Crater." Accessed November 7, 2021. https://mars.nasa.gov/mars2020/mission/science/landing-site/#:~:text=Jezero%20Crater%2C%20Mars%202020's%20Landing%20Site&text=Jezero%20Crater%20is%20thus%20likely,in%20the%20presence%20of%20water.

Average Temperature: 867°F (464°C): Barnett, Amanda. "Solar System Temperatures." NASA Solar System Exploration. Updated February 15, 2022. https://solarsystem.nasa.gov/resources/681/solar-system-temperatures/.

Venus is often referred: Choi, Charles Q., and Chelsea Gohd. "Venus: The Scorching Second Planet from the Sun." Space.com. March 31, 2022. https://www.space.com/44-venus-second-planet-from-the-sun-brightest-planet-in-solar-system.html#:~:text=Venus%20and%20Earth%20are%20often,miles%20(6%2C000%20km)%20wide.

Scientists believe Venus: Cabbage, Michael, and Leslie McCarthy. "NASA Climate Modeling Suggests Venus May Have Been Habitable." NASA. Updated August 6, 2017. https://www.nasa.gov/feature/goddard/2016/nasa-climate-modeling-suggests-venus-may-have-been-habitable.

Some think that certain chemicals: Stirone, Shannon, Kenneth Chang, and Dennis Overbye. "Life on Venus? Astronomers See a Signal in Its Clouds." *New York Times*. Updated June 22, 2021. https://www.nytimes.com/2020/09/14/science/venus-life-clouds.html.

One of Saturn's 82 moons: Barnett, Amanda. "Saturn Moons." NASA Solar System Exploration, Accessed November 7, 2021. https://solarsystem.nasa.gov/moons/saturn-moons/overview/?page=0&per_page=40&order=name+asc&search=&placeholder=Enter+moon+name&condition_1=38%3Aparent_id&condition_2=moon%3Abodytype%3Ailike&condition_3=moon%3Abody_type.

Small enough to fit: Choi, Charles Q. "A Porous Core May Heat the Ocean of Enceladus." *Scientific American*, November 7, 2017. https://www.scientificamerican.com/article/a-porous-core-may-heat-the-ocean-of-enceladus/#:~:text=Enceladus%20is%20only%20about%20314,and%20frozen%20solid%20by%20now.

Enceladus is one of: Patel, Neel V. "The Best Places to Find Extraterrestrial Life in Our Solar System, Ranked." *MIT Technology Review*. June 16, 2021. https://www.technologyreview.com/2021/06/16/1026473/best-worlds-extraterrestrial-life-solar-system-ranked/.

This is because of massive: Barnett, Amanda. "Enceladus." NASA Solar System Exploration. Updated December 19, 2019. https://solarsystem.nasa.gov/moons/saturn-moons/enceladus/in-depth/.

And where there's water: PBS News Hour. "Where There's Water on Earth, There's Life. Is the Same True on Mars?" September 28, 2015. https://www.pbs.org/newshour/show/water-mars.

One of Jupiter's: Barnett, Amanda. "Jupiter Moons." NASA Solar System Exploration. Accessed November 7, 2021. https://solarsystem.nasa.gov/moons/jupiter-moons/overview/?page=0&per_page=40&order=name+asc&search=&placeholder=Enter+moon+name&condition_1=9%3Aparent_id&condition_2=moon%3Abody_type%3Ailike&condition_3=moon%3Abody_type.

Discovered by Galileo: The Editors of Encyclopaedia Britannica. "Europa." *Encyclopaedia Britannica*. Accessed November 7, 2021. https://www.britannica.com/place/Europa-satellite-of-Jupiter.

That's the chemical: Thompson, Jay R. "Why Europa." NASA Europa Clipper. Accessed November 7, 2021. https://europa.nasa.gov/why-europa/ingredients-for-life/.

In 2012, researchers: NASA. "Hubble Space Telescope Sees Evidence of Water Vapor Venting off Jupiter Moon." December 12, 2013. https://www.nasa.gov/content/goddard/hubble-europa-water-vapor.

The Great Pyramids: Drake, Nadia. "7 Ancient Sites Some People Think Were Built by Aliens." *National Geographic*. October 26, 2017. https://www.nationalgeographic.com/travel/article/ancient-sites-built-by-aliens.

In fact, there have: Jarus, Owen. "A Ramp Contraption May Have Been Used to Build Egypt's Great Pyramid." *Scientific American*. November 5, 2018, https://www.scientificamerican.com/article/a-ramp-contraption-may-have-been-used-to-build-egypts-great-pyramid/.

In 1947, one: Ward, Alex, and Aja Romano. "Area 51 and Aliens: the Myth, the Meme, and the Strange Reality, Explained." *Vox*. September 19, 2019. https://www.vox.com/2019/9/19/20857221/storm-area-51-aliens-ufos-meme-myth-lore-history-bob-lazar-explained.

Although there is a military: The Editors of Encyclopaedia Britannica. "What Is Known (and Not Known) About Area 51." *Encyclopaedia Britannica*. Accessed November 7, 2021. https://www.britannica.com/story/what-is-known-and-not-known-about-area-51.

It was a weather: United States Air Force. "The Roswell Report." U.S. Department of Defense. 1995. https://media.defense.gov/2010/Dec/01/2001329893/-1/-1/0/roswell-2.pdf.

Must be calling cards: Radford, Benjamin, and Callum McKelvie. "Crop Circles: Myth, Theories and History." LiveScience. January 27, 2022. https://www.livescience.com/26540-crop-circles.html.

Most crop circles: Marks, Simon. "Crop Circle 'Inventor's' Son Talks about Father's Legacy." BBC News, September 7, 2019. https://www.bbc.com/news/av/uk-england-hampshire-49608647.

SETI is a nonprofit: SETI Institute. "History of the SETI Institute." Accessed November 7, 2021. https://www.seti.org/seti.

The scientists and astronomers: SETI Institute. "SETI Institute and National Radio Astronomy Observatory Team Up for SETI Science at the Very Large Array." SETI. February 13, 2020. https://www.seti.org/seti-institute-and-national-radio-astronomy-observatory-team-up-for-seti-science-at-very-large-array.

They do this to try: Freudenrich, Craig. "How SETI Works." HowStuffWorks.com. May 8, 2001. https://science.howstuffworks.com/seti.htm.

Kind of like scrolling: National Radio Astronomy Observatory. "The Technology of Radio Astronomy." Accessed November 7, 2021. https://public.nrao.edu/radio-astronomy/the-technology-of-radio-astronomy/.

Each radio and television signal: Starr, Michelle. "Mind-Boggling Image Shows How Far into Space Humanity's Voice Has Actually Reached." Sciencealert.com, April 21, 2019. https://www.sciencealert.com/humanity-hasn-t-reached-as-far-into-space-as-you-think.

Every broadcast we've: Qualitative Reasoning Group. "How does NASA Communicate with Spacecraft?" Northwestern University. Accessed November 7, 2021. https://www.qrg.northwestern.edu/projects/vss/docs/communications/2-why-does-it-take-so-long.html.

This means that: Cain, Fraser. "Are Aliens Watching Old TV Shows?" Universe Today. January 19, 2015. https://www.universetoday.com/118250/are-aliens-watching-old-tv-shows/.

Although this equation: Palma, Christopher. "The Drake Equation." The Pennsylvania State University. Accessed November 7, 2021. https://www.e-education.psu.edu/astro801/content/l12_p5.html.

Two golf balls: Royal Museums Greenwich. "The Strange Things We've Left on the Moon." Accessed November 7, 2021. https://www.rmg.co.uk/stories/topics/strange-things-humans-have-left-on-moon.

12 pairs of space boots: Stromberg, Joseph. "The 8 Weirdest Things We've Left on the Moon." *Vox*. March 8, 2015. https://www.vox.com/2015/3/8/8163259/moon-objects-weird.

In 1969, when Neil: Space.com Staff. "How Long Do Footprints Last on the Moon?" Space.com. March 1, 2012. https://www.space.com/14740-footprints-moon.html.

And with no wind, rain: Drake, Nadia. "Should Neil Armstrong's Bootprints Be on the Moon Forever?" *New York Times*. July 11, 2019. https://www.nytimes.com/2019/07/11/science/moon-apollo-11-archaeology-preservation.html.

A whole bunch: Zeidan, Adam. "What Have We Left on the Moon?" *Encyclopaedia Britannica*. Accessed November 7, 2021. https://www.britannica.com/story/what-have-we-left-on-the-moon#:~:text=Aside%20from%20trash%E2%80%94from%20food,that%20they%20no%20longer%20needed.

The Bible: Chodosh, Sara. "Money, Shoes, Poop, and Other Highlights from the 796 Items We've Left on the Moon." *Popular Science*. July 20, 2019. https://www.popsci.com/trash-items-left-on-moon-apollo-maps/.

96 bags: Resnick, Brian. "Apollo Astronauts Left Their Poop on the Moon." *Vox*. Updated July 12, 2019. https://www.vox.com/science-and-health/2019/3/22/18236125/apollo-moon-poop-mars-science.

A commemorative plaque: NASA Earth's Moon. "Apollo 11 Plaque." October 20, 2017. https://moon.nasa.gov/resources/136/apollo-11-plaque-/#:~:text=Armstrong%2C%20commander%2C%20and%20Edwin%20E,in%20peace%20for%20all%20mankind.%22.

Part of the Eagle lunar: NASA Space Science Data Coordinated Archive. "Apollo 11 Lunar Module." April 2022. https://nssdc.gsfc.nasa.gov/nmc/spacecraft/display.action?id=1969-059C.

Three lunar rovers: Heiney, Anna. "Apollo's Lunar Leftovers. NASA. June 28, 2004. https://www.nasa.gov/missions/solarsystem/f_leftovers.html.

Two medals: Smith, Kiona N. "The Apollo 11 Astronauts Left a Lot of Junk on the Moon." *Forbes*. July 20, 2017. https://www.forbes.com/sites/kionasmith/2017/07/20/the-apollo-11-astronauts-left-a-lot-of-junk-on-the-moon/?sh=4d4bd3464ca0.

aluminum sculpture called Fallen Astronaut: Barnett, Amanda. "Memorial to Fallen Astronauts on the Moon." NASA Solar System Exploration. Updated February 6, 2019. https://solarsystem.nasa.gov/resources/2279/memorial-to-fallen-astronauts-on-the-moon/.

One tiny silicon disc: NASA. "Apollo 11 Goodwill Messages." Accessed November 8, 2021. https://history.nasa.gov/ap11-35ann/goodwill/Apollo_11_material.pdf.

PART V: SPACE EXPLORATION

Gravity is what keeps us: Erickson, Kristen. "What Is Gravity?" NASA Space Place. December 17, 2020. https://spaceplace.nasa.gov/what-is-gravity/en/.

Robert Goddard is considered: NASA STEM Engagement. "A Pictorial History of Rockets." Accessed November 8, 2021. https://www.nasa.gov/sites/default/files/atoms/files/rockets-guide-20-history.pdf .

The largest spaceflight center: NASA History Program Office. "History of Goddard Space Flight Center." Last updated August 3, 2017. https://www.nasa.gov/offices/history/center_history/goddard_space_flight_center.

The space shuttle: Wild, Flint. "What Was the Space Shuttle?" NASA Knows! Last updated June 7, 2021. https://www.nasa.gov/audience/forstudents/5-8/features/nasa-knows/what-is-the-space-shuttle-58.html.

Today, most cargo: Wall, Mike. "Used SpaceX Dragon Cargo Ship Arrives at Space Station for Record 3rd Time." Space.com. July 27, 2019. https://www.space.com/spacex-dragon-cargo-ship-crs-18-arrives-space-station.html.

The Falcon 9: Logsdon, John M. "Falcon." *Encyclopaedia Britannica*, February 17, 2022. https://www.britannica.com/technology/Titan-rocket.

A company called Lockheed Martin: Lockheed Martin Corporation. "Orion." Accessed November 8, 2021. https://www.lockheedmartin.com/en-us/products/orion.html.

At a height of 150,000 feet (45,720 meters): Brown, Irene. "Solid Rocket Boosters." Encyclopedia.com. Accessed June 16, 2022. https://www.encyclopedia.com/science/news-wires-white-papers-and-books/solid-rocket-boosters.

Once in orbit: Ryba, Jeanne. "Extended Duration Missions." NASA. Last updated April 11, 2008. https://www.nasa.gov/mission_pages/shuttle/launch/extend_duration.html#:~:text=Typical%20shuttle%20flights%20last%20about,approximately%2016%20days%20in%20length.

The longest mission: Tillman, Nola Taylor. "The First Space Shuttle Flight into Space." Space.com. May 7, 2019. https://www.space.com/16793-first-space-shuttle-launch.html.

When it's time to come: The Aerospace Corporation. "Did I See a Meteor or a Reentry?" Accessed November 8, 2021. https://aerospace.org/article/what-does-reentry-look-like#:~:text=It%20is%20usually%20moving%20parallel,any%20time%20of%20the%20day.

There are only 58 years: National Air and Space Museum. "Inventing a Flying Machine." Accessed November 8, 2021. https://airandspace.si.edu/exhibitions/wright-brothers/online/fly/1903/.

Experience Earth from 250 miles (402 km): Wild, Flint. "What Is the International Space Station?" NASA Knows! October 30, 2020. https://www.nasa.gov/audience/forstudents/k-4/stories/nasa-knows/what-is-the-iss-k4.html.

That's 35 times higher: Pilot Institute. "How High Do Planes Fly? Airplane Flight Altitude." August 27, 2021. https://pilotinstitute.com/airplane-height/.

With the help of 15 nations: Garcia, Mark. "International Cooperation." NASA International Space Station. Last updated October 15, 2020. https://www.nasa.gov/mission_pages/station/cooperation/index.html.

And a rotating carousel: ISS National Laboratory. "History and Timeline of the ISS." Accessed November 9, 2021. https://www.issnationallab.org/about/iss-timeline/.

You'll have plenty of room: Garcia, Mark. "International Space Station Facts and Figures." NASA. November 4, 2021. https://www.nasa.gov/feature/facts-and-figures.

Say goodbye to the 65 miles (105 km): Federal Highway Administration. "The Safety Impacts of Differential Speed Limits on Rural Interstate Highways." Techbrief. September 2004. https://www.fhwa.dot.gov/publications/research/safety/04156/index.cfm.

Enjoy three packaged meals a day: May, Sandra. "Eating in Space." NASA. June 27, 2018. https://www.nasa.gov/audience/foreducators/stem-on-station/ditl_eating.

from a robust menu of over 200: Feltman, Rachel. "Ever Wondered What's on the Astronauts' Menu?" *The Washington Post*. November 7, 2018. https://www.washingtonpost.com/lifestyle/kidspost/ever-wondered-whats-on-the-astronauts-menu/2018/11/02/cf9afbd0-c34d-11e8-b338-a3289f6cb742_story.html.

NASA spent $23 million: Elburn, Darcy. "Boldly Go! NASA's New Space Toilet Offers More Comfort, Improved Efficiency for Deep Space Missions." NASA Moon to Mars. Last updated September 24, 2020. https://www.nasa.gov/feature/boldly -go-nasa-s-new-space-toilet-offers-more-comfort-improved-efficiency-for-deep-space.

Check out our state-of-the-art: NASA Tumblr. "Exercising in Space." January 5, 2016. https://nasa.tumblr.com/ post/136706596374/exercising-in-space.

Space walks not included: Wild, Flint. "What Is a Spacewalk?" NASA Knows! July 27, 2020. https://www.nasa.gov/ audience/forstudents/k-4/stories/nasa-knows/what-is-a-spacewalk-k4.html.

Boil your bodily fluids!: NASA Museum in a Box. "Why Do We Really Need Pressure Suits?" Accessed November 9, 2021. https://www.nasa.gov/sites/default/files/atoms/files/dressing_for_altitude.pdf

Freeze your nose and mouth off: Kwan, Jacklin. "What Would Happen to the Human Body in the Vacuum of Space?" LiveScience. November 13, 2021. https://www.livescience.com/human-body-no-spacesuit.

in temperatures of −455 degrees F: Springel, Mark. "The Human Body in Space: Distinguishing Fact from Fiction." Harvard University Graduate School of Arts and Sciences. July 30, 2013. https://sitn.hms.harvard.edu/flash/2013/ space-human-body/.

Dodge micrometeoroids: Corbett, Judy. "Micrometeoroids and Orbital Debris (MMOD)." NASA. Last updated August 6, 2017. https://www.nasa.gov/centers/wstf/site_tour/remote_hypervelocity_test_laboratory/micrometeoroid_and_ orbital_debris.html.

Enjoy the sensation: Ludacer, Rob, and David Anderson. "How Long Humans Could Survive in Space without a Space-suit." *Business Insider.* May 13, 2021. https://www.businessinsider.com/how-long-human-survive-outer-space-without -spacesuit-2017-5#:~:text=The%20vacuum%20of%20space%20will,but%20you%20won't%20explode.

The good news is that scientists: Cadogan, David P. "The Past and Future Space Suit." *American Scientist.* Accessed November 9, 2021. https://www.americanscientist.org/article/the-past-and-future-space-suit.

13 layers!: Freudenrich, Craig. "How Space Suits Work." HowStuffWorks.com. December 14, 2000. https://science .howstuffworks.com/space-suit.htm.

Takes only 45 minutes to put on!: NASA Spacesuits and Spacewalks. "Facts About Spacesuits and Spacewalking." Last updated July 5, 2018. https://www.nasa.gov/audience/foreducators/spacesuits/facts/index.html#:~:text=A%20 spacesuit%20weighs%20approximately%20280,that%20help%20keep%20astronauts%20cool.

Space Adaptation Syndrome: APA Dictionary of Psychology. "Space Adaptation Syndrome." Accessed November 9, 2021. https://dictionary.apa.org/space-adaptation-syndrome.

In space, your body could grow: Kramer, Miriam. "Strange but True: Astronauts Get Taller in Space." *Scientific American.* January 7, 2013. https://www.scientificamerican.com/article/astronauts-get-taller-in-space/#:~:text= Astronauts%20in%20space%20can%20grow,5%20centimeters)%20while%20in%20orbit.

Without Earth's gravity: Canright, Shelley. "My How You've Grown!" NASAexplores. Last updated April 9, 2009. https://www.nasa.gov/audience/forstudents/5-8/features/F_How_Youve_Grown_5-8.html.

Your body responds by: Gregg, Tracy. "How Do Astronauts Go to the Bathroom in Space?" University at Buffalo NOW. March 23, 2021. https://www.buffalo.edu/ubnow/stories/2021/03/gregg-conversation-bathroom-space.html.

So don't be surprised if: Canright, Shelley. "Human Vestibular System in Space." NASAexplores. Last updated April 10, 2009. https://www.nasa.gov/audience/forstudents/9-12/features/F_Human_Vestibular_System_in_Space.html.

But don't worry: Gaskill, Melissa. "International Space Station Research Keeps an Eye on Vision Changes in Space." NASA International Space Station Program Research Office. Last updated September 23, 2020. https://www.nasa.gov/ mission_pages/station/research/news/iss-20-evolution-of-vision-research.

That's why it's important: Lyndon B. Johnson Space Center. "Muscle Atrophy." NASA Information, Accessed November 9, 2021. https://www.nasa.gov/pdf/64249main_ffs_factsheets_hbp_atrophy.pdf.

No one for sure knows why: Canadian Space Agency. "Sleeping in Space." Government of Canada. Modified August 22, 2019. https://www.asc-csa.gc.ca/eng/astronauts/living-in-space/sleeping-in-space.asp.

In other words, 24 hours: Archer, Simon, and Derk-Jan Dijk. "Getting to Sleep in Space Is Hard—and Not Exactly Restful for the Mind and Body." *The Conversation.* June 22, 2016. https://theconversation.com/getting-to-sleep-in -space-is-hard-and-not-exactly-restful-for-the-mind-and-body-61445.

This makes it hard: Elliott, Ann R., Steven A. Shea, Derk-Jan Dijk et al. "Microgravity Reduces Sleep-Disordered Breathing in Humans." *American Journal of Respiratory and Critical Care Medicine* 164, no. 3 (August 1, 2001): 478–485. https://www.atsjournals.org/doi/full/10.1164/ajrccm.164.3.2010081.

This is so common: Jaggard, Victoria. "Astronauts' Fingernails Falling Off Due to Glove Design." *National Geographic.* September 14, 2010. https://www.nationalgeographic.com/culture/article/100913-science-space-astronauts-gloves -fingernails-injury?loggedin=true.

Innovations originally designed: Green, Josie. "Inventions We Use Every Day That Were Actually Created for Space Exploration." *USA Today*. Updated July 8, 2019. https://www.usatoday.com/story/money/2019/07/08/space-race -inventions-we-use-every-day-were-created-for-space-exploration/39580591/.

This digitally altered photo: Malik, Tariq. "Astronauts 'Spacewalk' Without Spacesuits in Cosmic Prank." Space .com. April 1, 2010. https://www.space.com/8130-astronauts-spacewalk-spacesuits-cosmic-prank.html.

Just as fellow astronaut Tim: Gittins, William. "How Astronaut Twins Smuggled a Gorilla Suit Aboard the ISS." AS .com. January 11, 2022. https://en.as.com/en/2022/01/11/latest_news/1641907819_601071.html.

PART V: SPACE SAILORS

Do You Have What It Takes?: NASA STEM Engagement. "How to Be an Astronaut." Accessed November 9, 2021. https://www.nasa.gov/stem-ed-resources/how-to-be-an-astronaut.html.

Do you have at least 1,000: Deiss, Heather. "Astronaut Requirements." NASA. Updated January 14, 2022. https:// www.nasa.gov/audience/forstudents/postsecondary/features/F_Astronaut_Requirements.html.

Are you between 62: carylsue. "NASA Wants You!" *National Geographic* (education blog). November 5, 2015. https:// blog.education.nationalgeographic.org/2015/11/05/nasa-wants-you/.

Astronauts aboard the International Space Station: Orr, Kim. "Our Favorite Projects for Summertime STEAM." NASA Jet Propulsion Laboratory Edu News. May 31, 2022. https://www.jpl.nasa.gov/edu/news/2022/5/31/our-favorite -projects-for-summertime-steam/.

Welcome to Astronaut School: Canright, Shelley. "Astronauts in Training." NASA Education. April 9, 2009. https:// www.nasa.gov/audience/forstudents/5-8/features/F_Astronauts_in_Training.html#:~:text=It%20can%20take%20 up%20to,NASA%20T%2D38%20training%20jets.&text=Astronauts%20also%20take%20classes.

All astronauts must be able: Howell, Elizabeth. "Want to be an Astronaut? Learn How to Speak Russian." *Universe Today*. April 8, 2013. https://www.universetoday.com/101302/want-to-be-an-astronaut-learn-how-to-speak-russian/.

A life-size model: Kauderer, Amiko. "Extreme Makeover—Space Vehicle Mockup Facility." NASA Johnson Space Center. Last updated December 17, 2012. https://www.nasa.gov/centers/johnson/home/extreme_makeover_svmf.html.

Typical training sessions: Petty, John Ira. "Zero-Gravity Plane on Final Flight." NASA. Last updated November 30, 2007. https://www.nasa.gov/vision/space/preparingtravel/kc135onfinal.html.

In March 2020: Blodgett, Rachael. "Application Procedures for Astronaut Candidate Program." NASA. Last updated April 1, 2020. https://www.nasa.gov/feature/application-procedures-for-astronaut-candidate-program/.

and only picked 10: Margetta, Robert. "NASA Selects New Astronaut Recruits to Train for Future Missions." NASA Humans in Space. Last updated February 1, 2022. https://www.nasa.gov/press-release/nasa-selects-new-astronaut -recruits-to-train-for-future-missions.

An astronaut's workday: Canright, Shelley. "An Astronaut's Work." NASA Student Features. Last updated April 10, 2009. https://www.nasa.gov/audience/forstudents/9-12/features/F_Astronauts_Work.html.

back at NASA's mission control: Space Center Houston. "International Space Station Mission Control." Accessed November 9, 2021. https://spacecenter.org/exhibits-and-experiences/nasa-tram-tour/new-mission-control/.

Time to unstrap myself: May, Sandra. "Sleeping in Space." NASA. Last updated April 28, 2021. https://www.nasa.gov/ audience/foreducators/stem-on-station/ditl_sleeping.

Upon waking, I spend: May, Sandra. "Morning Routine in Space." NASA. Last updated April 28, 2021. https://www .nasa.gov/audience/foreducators/stem-on-station/ditl_morning_routine.

What's with all these straps: Elburn, Darcy. "Boldly Go! NASA's New Space Toilet Offers More Comfort, Improved Efficiency for Deep Space Missions." NASA Moon to Mars. Last updated September 24, 2020. https://www.nasa.gov/ feature/boldly-go-nasa-s-new-space-toilet-offers-more-comfort-improved-efficiency-for-deep-space.

Sometimes astronaut poop: Gregg, Tracy. "How Do Astronauts Go to the Bathroom in Space?" University at Buffalo Now. March 23, 2021. https://www.buffalo.edu/ubnow/stories/2021/03/gregg-conversation-bathroom-space.

In 2018, NASA spent $23 million: Thompson, Amy. "NASA Just Sent a New $23 Million Space Toilet to the International Space Station." *Smithsonian Magazine*. October 9, 2020. https://www.smithsonianmag.com/science-nature/nasa-just -sent-new-23-million-space-toilet-international-space-station-180976037/.

And by "shower": Wong, Caleb. "How to Shower in Space." National Air and Space Museum. July 18, 2017. https:// airandspace.si.edu/stories/editorial/how-shower-space.

That includes the moisture: Wiedemann, Darlene. "Water Recycling." NASA Exploration: Beyond Earth. Last updated October 16, 2014. https://www.nasa.gov/content/water-recycling/.

A nutritionist on Earth: May, Sandra. "Eating in Space." NASA. Last updated April 28, 2021. https://www.nasa.gov/ audience/foreducators/stem-on-station/ditl_eating.

This packaging is flexible: Royal Museums Greenwich. "What Do Astronauts Eat in Space?" Accessed November 9, 2021. https://www.rmg.co.uk/stories/topics/what-do-astronauts-eat-space.

Some food can be eaten: National Air and Space Museum. "Space Food, Seasoned Scrambled Eggs, STS-27." Accessed November 9, 2021. https://airandspace.si.edu/collection-objects/space-food-seasoned-scrambled-eggs -sts-27/nasm_A19890270000.

In order eat it: BBC. "How to Make Scrambled Eggs in Space." Newsround. January 31, 2016. https://www.bbc.co.uk/ newsround/35454548.

Think of us the next: NASA Education. "Salt and Pepper Dispensers (2007)." Last updated July 7, 2014. https:// www.nasa.gov/audience/forstudents/k-4/stories/salt-and-pepper-dispensers.html#:~:text=NASA%20LOCATIONS& text=If%20astronauts%20sprinkled%20salt%20and,pepper%20in%20a%20liquid%20form.

There is no refrigerator: Wiles, Kayla. "To Give Astronauts Better Food, Engineers Test a Fridge Prototype in Microgravity." *Purdue University News*. May 27, 2021. https://www.purdue.edu/newsroom/releases/2021/Q2/to-give -astronauts-better-food,-engineers-test-a-fridge-prototype-in-microgravity.html.

Several labs: Zehnder, Jeff. "New FRIDGE Could Bring Real Ice Cream to Space." University of Colorado Boulder Ann and H.J. Smead Aerospace Engineering Sciences. April 23, 2020. https://www.colorado.edu/aerospace/2020/04/23/ new-fridge-could-bring-real-ice-cream-space#:~:text=NASA%20has%20ordered%20eight%20FRIDGE,station%20 while%20awaiting%20active%20research.

The cookies were part: Dunn, Marcia. "First Space-Baked Cookies Took 2 Hours in Experimental Oven." *AP News*. January 22, 2020. https://apnews.com/article/us-news-ap-top-news-tx-state-wire-oddities-science-7f30aa7b8f073a6f 12bdb2528f3eec88.

It was a gift from Italy: News.Italianfood.net. "Isspresso Gets Back from Space." December 18, 2017. https://news .italianfood.net/2017/12/18/isspresso-gets-back-space/.

Corn Chowder: National Air and Space Museum. "Space Food, Corn Chowder, Apollo 16." Accessed November 9, 2021. https://airandspace.si.edu/collection-objects/space-food-corn-chowder-apollo-16/nasm_A19980131000.

Shrimp Cocktail: NASA SpaceLink. "Space and Food Nutrition: An Educator's Guide with Activities in Science and Mathematics." Accessed November 9, 2021. https://www.nasa.gov/pdf/143163main_Space.Food.and.Nutrition.pdf

And since there's no up or down: May, Sandra. "Sleeping in Space." NASA. Last updated April 28, 2021. https://www .nasa.gov/audience/foreducators/stem-on-station/ditl_sleeping.

Equipped with a patch: Soniak, Matt. "How Do Astronauts Scratch Their Noses on Space Walks?" *Mental Floss*. October 3, 2013. https://www.mentalfloss.com/article/52987/how-do-astronauts-scratch-their-noses-space-walks.

The EVA is tough: Jones, Eric M., and Ken Glover (eds.). "Lunar Extravehicular Visor Assembly (LEVA)." *Apollo Lunar Surface Journal*. NASA. June 12, 2011. https://www.hq.nasa.gov/alsj/alsj-LEVA.html.

Just poop and pee: NASA Education. "Learn About Spacesuits." Last updated May 29, 2014. https://www.nasa.gov/ audience/foreducators/spacesuits/home/clickable_suit_nf.html.

EMU Electrical Harness: Freudenrich, Craig. "How Space Suits Work." HowStuffWorks.com. December 14, 2000. https://science.howstuffworks.com/space-suit.htm.

Complete with a cheat sheet: NASASpaceLink. "Suited for Spacewalking—A Teacher's Guide with Activities for Technology Education, Mathematics, and Science." Accessed November 9, 2021. https://www.nasa.gov/pdf/ 143159main_Suited_for_Spacewalking.pdf

And they rode there: Pearlman, Robert Z. "LEGO Figures Flying on NASA Jupiter Probe." Space.com. August 4, 2011. www.space.com/12546-lego-figures-jupiter-juno-spacecraft.html.

This timeless album: NASA Jet Propulsion Laboratory: Voyager. "What Are the Contents of the Golden Record?" Accessed November 9, 2021. https://voyager.jpl.nasa.gov/golden-record/whats-on-the-record/.

Bread isn't allowed in space: Howell, Elizabeth. "How John Young Smuggled a Corned-Beef Sandwich into Space." Space.com. January 10, 2018. https://www.space.com/39341-john-young-smuggled-corned-beef-space.html.

The first woman to fly: Pearlman, Robert Z. "Amelia Earhart's Watch Reaches Space Station 82 Years After Historic Flight." Space.com. June 18, 2010. https://www.space.com/8631-amelia-earhart-watch-reaches-space-station-82-years -historic-flight.html.

It should also be noted: NASA. "Astronauts to Fly Amelia Earhart Watch. Scarf." Last updated November 14, 2013. https://www.nasa.gov/mission_pages/station/expeditions/expedition24/earhart_watch.html.

This original lightsaber: Whitesides, Loretta Hidalgo. "Skywalkers' Lightsaber to Fly on Space Shuttle." *Wired*. August 20, 2007. https://www.wired.com/2007/08/skywalkers-ligh/.

In fact, they never: Siceloff, Steven. "Items Taken into Space Reflect Accomplishments on Earth." NASA Missions Behind the Scenes. Last updated November 23, 2007. https://www.nasa.gov/mission_pages/shuttle/behindscenes/Whatsgoingup.html.

But what do you do: Wild, Flint. "What Is the International Space Station?" NASA Knows! Last updated November 2, 2020. https://www.nasa.gov/audience/forstudents/k-4/stories/nasa-knows/what-is-the-iss-k4.html.

While the pizza only cost: BBC News. "Pizza Sets New Delivery Record." May 22, 2001. http://news.bbc.co.uk/2/hi/americas/1345139.stm.

To mark the first launch: Molina, Brett. "A Tesla Roadster in Orbit. A 'Starman' at the Wheel. Why This Incredible Image Has Us Excited about Space Exploration." *USA Today*, Updated February 8, 2018. https://www.usatoday.com/story/tech/news/2018/02/07/tesla-roadster-orbit-starman-wheel-why-incredible-image-has-us-excited-space-exploration/314502002/.

It's been traveling: Puiu, Tibi. "Four Years Ago, Elon Musk Sent a Tesla to Space. What Happened to It?" *ZME Science*. February 9, 2022. https://www.zmescience.com/science/four-years-ago-elon-musk-sent-a-tesla-to-space-what-happened-to-it/.

The goal is to eventually: Harbaugh, Jennifer. "Space Station 3-D Printer Builds Ratchet Wrench to Complete First Phase of Operations." NASA. Last updated August 7, 2017. https://www.nasa.gov/mission_pages/station/research/news/3Dratchet_wrench.

Robonaut lives on the ISS: Wild, Flint. "What Is Robonaut?" NASA Knows! April 10, 2019. https://www.nasa.gov/audience/forstudents/5-8/features/nasa-knows/what-is-robonaut-58.html.

It's remote-controlled: Editorial Staff. "11 Amazing Gadgets You'll Find on the International Space Station." *Mental Floss*. July 8, 2015. https://www.mentalfloss.com/article/65013/11-amazing-gadgets-youll-find-international-space-station.

In 2014, Robonaut: NASA. "Lower Limbs for Robonaut 2 Are Aboard the International Space Station." Phys.org. April 25, 2014. https://phys.org/news/2014-04-limbs-robonaut-aboard-international-space.html.

Put on weight: NASA and Texas Instruments. "ARED—Resistive Exercise in Space." Math and Science @ Work. Accessed November 9, 2021. /https://www.nasa.gov/pdf/553871main_AP_ST_Phys_ARED.pdf.

There's also a treadmill: Kauderer, Amiko. "Do Tread on Me." NASA International Space Station. Last updated October 23, 2010. https://www.nasa.gov/mission_pages/station/behindscenes/colbert_feature.html.

Made in Canada: Garcia, Mark. "Mobile Servicing System Overview." NASA International Space Station. Last updated November 16, 2018. https://www.nasa.gov/mission_pages/station/structure/elements/mobile-servicing-system.html.

The Canadarm: Kauderer, Amiko. "Space Station Assembly." NASA International Space Station. Last updated January 8, 2013. https://www.nasa.gov/mission_pages/station/structure/elements/subsystems.html.

Launched in 2008: Siceloff, Steven. "Recycling Water Is Not Just for Earth Anymore." NASA International Space Station Behind the Scenes. October 23, 2010. https://www.nasa.gov/mission_pages/station/behindscenes/waterrecycler.html.

PHOTO CREDITS

19 STUDIO/Shutterstock: 18, 22, 23, 24, 25, 26, 28, 29, 30, 31

24K-Production/Shutterstock: 41

Artsiom P/Shutterstock: 20

M.Aurelius/Shutterstock: 121

CloudOnePhoto/Shutterstock: 89 (top)

Dan Breckwoldt/Shutterstock: 88

brichuas/Shutterstock: 71

Dotted Yeti/Shutterstock: 86, 87 (top)

Daniel Fung/Shutterstock: 32–34

Everett Collection/Shutterstock: 70

Jeff Lueders/Shutterstock: 126

muratart/Shutterstock: 92–93

Robert Hoetink/Shutterstock: 89 (bottom)

Lia Koltyrina/Shutterstock: 21

NASA: 37, 38, 67

Nazarii_Neshcherenskyi/Shutterstock: 19

Nerthuz/Shutterstock: 27, 131

Alex Terentii/Shutterstock: 40

Whitelion61 Shutterstock: 87 (bottom)

INDEX

THE THANK-YOU PAGE

WAIT! WAIT! WAIT! We're not finished here! Before you close this book, we'd like to dump a bunch of cosmic confetti on the people who helped us make it.

First and foremost, a huge shout-out to our longtime WOW collaborator, Tom van Kalken. Your space dust is sprinkled throughout these pages, and it's been an absolute blast scheming, dreaming, writing, wondering, and wowing with you!

We also want to give a galactic amount of gratitude and appreciation to our visionary illustrator, Mike Centeno, and our incredible design duo, Corina Lupp and Alison Klapthor. What a dream collaboration team! Thank you for making this book such a vibrant, fun, visual delight!

Five stars to our diligent fact-checker, Rachael Lallensack. Your attention to detail and enthusiasm have helped us create a book that's both factual and fun.

Our editor, Amy Cloud, is a shining star in our galaxy of Wow in the World books. Amy, your passion, guidance, and vision have helped us create the books we wanted to read as kids, and it's an absolute joy to share this with you.

To the amazing team at Clarion Books and HarperCollins Publishers—Mary Magrisso, Joan L. Giurdanella, Susan Bishansky, Melissa Cicchitelli, John Sellers, and Sabrina Abballe—thank you for your unwavering support and dedication to launching our books into the hands of young readers.

We owe a cargo ship of gratitude to our literary agent, Steven Malk. Your support and guidance from the very beginning have helped us to reach beyond the stars.

And while this book might be for your eyeballs, our *Wow in the World* podcast is for your earballs! And with that, we'd like to thank our galactically talented team at Tinkercast, who help to make everything you see and hear from us possible: Jed Anderson, Tyler Tholl, Tom van Kalken, Jodi Nussbaum, Steph Sosa, Henry Moskal, Jessica Boddy, Rebecca Caban, Kenny Curtis, Johanna Weber, Anna Zagorski, Twee Mac, Natascha Crandall, Ruth Morrison, Sana Alimohamed, Lizzie Freilich, Kristen Giang, Kyle Alston, Ali Paksima, Linda Rothenberg, Kit Ballenger, Jason Rabinowitz, Jacob Stein, and of course, our number one partner in wow, Meredith Halpern-Ranzer.

We'd also like to thank our wonderful partners at our home planet, Wondery Media. We're so proud to be part of your universe!

But wait—there's one more person we can't forget to thank! That's right, YOU! We launched this book into the stratosphere with the hope that it would land in your hands, and we're so grateful that it did. Thank you for being a part of our cosmic adventure.

Now close this book and get outside to discover some WOW in your world and beyond!

—Mindy and Guy